Staying Home With The Kids

HOW TO STAY SANE, STAY 'YOU' AND
ENJOY YOUR TIME AT HOME WITH
YOUR LITTLE PEOPLE

Nicola Semple

http://nicolasemple.com

ACKNOWLEDGEMENTS

I'd like to thank the mums who took the time to share their experiences and contribute to *Staying Home With The Kids*. Some of them have been mentioned by name; others have chosen to remain anonymous. All of them are doing great things for their family each and every day.

To the 'ladies with the red pens' who read the early versions of this book. Your precision and insights helped make *Staying Home With The Kids* better than I could ever have made it on my own.

To my support crew, the fabulous ladies who have kept me going over the past few years. Each of you is carving your own (very different) path on this journey of motherhood and giving me your unfaltering support along the way.

To Mum and Dad, without you I wouldn't be where I am today.

To W, for always, always believing in me, even when I don't believe in myself.

And finally to my little people, Super Girl and Boy Wonder. May you continue to be the happy, curious, life-loving souls that you are. We love you more than you can imagine (until you have little people of your own and then you will get it).

Staying Home With The Kids

Contents

About The Author 1

Introduction... 5

What's the Big Deal Anyway?.. 13

The Decision to Stay at Home.. 23

The Reality of Being Home with the Kids 45

How to Save Your Sanity 65

Money, Money, Money… 83

Your Relationships... 99

Your Confidence 107

Look After Yourself 117

Future-Proof Yourself 127

Start Your Own Business 137

And This Too Shall Pass.. 151

About The Author

My name is Nicola and I'm a stay-at-home mum. I look after my two children: Super Girl, who's five and a half (the half being very important to her!) at the time of writing, and Boy Wonder, who is three. As well as looking after my own family, I work with women wanting to build a business around their kids; I give them the encouragement, motivation and skills they need to be successful.

I'm the most unlikely stay-at-home mum you could possibly imagine. I spent my teenage years and early twenties gathering a clutch of qualifications – an Honours degree in International Business, a Masters in Organisational Behaviour and a professional qualification in Personnel and Development. Then I spent 10 years working as a business change consultant. Long hours and constant travel were the norm. Life was good and full of achievements. I had absolutely no desire to have children, never mind stay at home and look after them myself.

1

I can still clearly recall a conversation I had with my best friend when I was 19. She told me that when she 'grew up' she was going to get married and have two boys (which she now has). I couldn't even begin to imagine why she would want to have children. We had the world at our feet; so much to see and so much to do. Why would we want to be tied down looking after babies?

She, along with every other person I spoke to about my lack of desire to have children, said, "You'll change your mind. You'll see". I always thought, "I hope I do because I'd love to understand what you're on about".

And of course, they were right. I got to my late 20s and started thinking, "Mmm, maybe they have a point. Maybe having children really is what life's all about". The crunch point came on a holiday to New York when my husband and I agreed that, although we'd had a lot of fun, we were ready for a change of pace. And that meant a change of focus.

This was probably just as well, because shortly after we got back we discovered that I was pregnant. Poor Super Girl spent the very first few days of her existence being pickled in New York's finest cocktail bars. She has never shown any ill-effects, but I'll be looking out for a penchant for Dirty Martinis later on in life.

For me, the decision to stay at home was almost instant, when Super Girl was born. Everybody assumed that I would find a nursery or nanny (or both) and carry on as I had before. In truth, I'd have probably needed both, given the long hours and travel that my former work required.

Pretty much straight away, though, I knew I didn't want life to be like that. I'd watched women return to work after maternity leave: they were constantly stretched and always apologising for leaving the office 'early' to go home and relieve whoever was looking after their child. They snatched pockets of time with their children in the evenings before getting back on their laptop for the night shift. They all told me they didn't have a choice. They couldn't possibly afford to stay at home, they said. While the situation wasn't ideal, it would only be for a few years; then the kids would be at school and it would all get easier... Wouldn't it?

I wasn't convinced. What was the point of bringing these little people into the world, if you were going to spend large parts of the time working to pay for others to look after them? Surely there had to be another way?

And there is another way. It requires sacrifice and the willingness to take a path you never expected to take. But there definitely is another way. I encourage you to view this as a choice. If going back to work is what you want to do and if it suits your family, then go for it! It will be a juggling act, but there are some fantastic role models who are successfully managing to combine a traditional career with bringing up children. If, however, you don't want to go back to your old job, then I want you to be brave. Giving up your role can be a daunting prospect, particularly in today's society where so much value is placed on our job and the status that comes with it. The financial implications can also be overwhelming; giving up on the security of a steady income is not for the faint-hearted. You have to have the confidence to go for it. But I urge you to grab that opportunity. Your little people will only be little for a short time. Make the most of it!

Introduction

"Strong Women: May we know them, May we be them, May we raise them."

Unknown

The widely accepted, modern-day definition of a strong woman is a multitasking whirlwind who, spurred on by Sheryl Sandberg's call to 'lean in', juggles career and family. This Wonder Woman spins all of the plates of modern life and is a gym-going, green smoothie-drinking fashion icon who has it all. Or does she? Does this strong woman really exist or is she an amalgamation of all of our insecurities and the media's interpretation of the type of woman that we 'should' strive to be?

I've discovered that there's a different kind of strong woman out there, one who fits a very different mould. And she is real. You'll find her at the park discovering leaves with her pre-schooler, crawling around and building sandcastles with her four-year-old and at toddler groups calming a fractious toddler while feeding her newborn. You'll find her at the school gates handing over water bottles, homework books and PE bags. And these days, you'll also find her at the growing number of child-friendly business networking meetings discussing the pros and cons of marketing on Facebook while bouncing a baby on her knee.

These women are everywhere, but to the uninitiated they are 'just' mums. And as such, they aren't particularly interesting. They 'just' stay at home to look after their children and their worlds revolve around nappies, snack times and the school run.

Look a bit closer, though, and you'll find that these women are the brave ones. In a world where we are being encouraged more and more strongly to hand over our children to nannies and nurseries so that we can make a contribution as an employee, these women are choosing another path. They have decided to live life differently; they have decided to live the life they think is right for their family.

I want to be clear from the outset. This book is not an attack on working mothers. Some women work because they have no choice and others work because they love the variety and stimulation that paid work gives them. I firmly believe that every woman and every family should have the right to create a lifestyle that works for them. We should not underestimate the Herculean task of keeping an employer and a family happy at the same time. Mums who return to their career do an amazing job of juggling their work commitments and the needs of everyone at home.

What I want to do, though, is to give a voice to the thousands and thousands of mothers who have decided they do want to look after their children themselves; the women who decide to not return to work after maternity leave because they want to stay at home and do this important job. They are a lost swathe of our population; they are the forgotten masses who work tirelessly day in, day out with no financial reward and little recognition outside the four walls of their home. To these women I say, "Ladies, you've not been forgotten. I see you. You matter. The work that you do every day makes a difference to those closest to you. And while it may not always feel like it, they love and appreciate you for it."

While being at home with your children may be hugely rewarding overall, the day-to-day reality can be rocky at times. In *Staying Home With The Kids*, I want to acknowledge some of the challenges that you'll face as a stay-at-home mum so you know you are not alone. I also want to provide some advice based on my own experience and the experiences of other mums about how to make the daily reality of staying home with the kids more rewarding and positive.

What about the dads?

This book has been written for mums but I acknowledge the rising number of dads staying at home to look after their children. And what a great trend that is! We should celebrate the fact that more children have an adult who loves them looking after them. Some of the themes and issues identified in this book may well resonate with stay-at-home dads, but I believe they face their own particular set of issues. As such, I suggest checking out some of the great resources available for stay-at-home dads at http://athomedad.org and http://stayathomedads.co.uk

What to expect in this book

I wanted to write *Staying Home With The Kids* because I was genuinely surprised by how few books there were about being a stay-at-home mum. When I decided to stay at home with my children, I approached it in the only way I knew how: I set about educating myself on what life would be like and what I'd let myself in for. And I found plenty of books. Some were (rather old-fashioned) handbooks on 'running a good home'. Others celebrated motherhood and the phenomenally important role a mother plays in the life of her offspring. Some simply gave advice on managing family life on a budget. I discovered an enormous number of books on how to generate an income from home. Believe me, there are *a lot* of these. If only we could all run six-figure businesses in nap time, the world would be a wonderful place! I also found lots of 'mummy blogs' where bloggers told their own personal story of looking after their children. Some were playing for laughs. Others were influenced by the desire to attract lucrative sponsorship deals. And who can blame them? Blogging has become a great way for women to generate additional income and still be around for their kids.

What I didn't find were the cold hard facts – and I'm a cold hard facts kinda girl. What was life going to be like?

What would be the challenges and the rewards? What were people going to think? I guess with hindsight (and now that my analytical, corporate brain has had six years to decompress and reacclimatise to the real world) it's clear that nobody could have ever completely answered those questions for me. Even so, a few pointers here and there would've been welcome.

That's one of the main reasons I felt compelled to write this book. I'd like to offer the kind of support that I'd have appreciated when I was about to become a new stay-at-home mum. I want to provide both information **and** the benefit of my own experience to those new mothers who are following on behind me – the mums who are trying to decide if looking after their children full-time is the right answer for them, as well as the mums already living with the day-to-day reality of caring for their children. I've written the book that reassures mums that it's okay to stay at home and look after their children if that's what they want, a book that also acknowledges the day-to-day challenges of what it means to make that choice.

In this book, we will cover:

Chapter 1: What's the Big Deal Anyway? Mothers have been looking after their children for thousands of years and will continue to do so for thousands more. So why is the decision to give up work and stay home with your children even a topic worthy of discussion? In this chapter, we explore some of the changes in modern society that mean staying at home with your kids is now considered the exception rather than the norm.

Chapter 2: The Decision to Stay at Home. The decision to stay at home is complex and needs to take into account some practicalities (for example, your finances) as well as the type of childhood that you want your children to have. In this chapter, we look at some of the issues that you might want to take into consideration when deciding if staying at home with your children is the right fit for you and your family.

Chapter 3: The Reality of Being Home with the Kids. What is it really like to be at home with your children full-time? In the early days, it's all about feeding and weaning, helping them take those tentative first steps and learning to talk, and guiding your little one to navigate the world around them. Later, the issues centre on the constraints of the school day and holidays, dealing with teachers and the school system. In this chapter, we cover what day-to-day life is like when you are a full-time carer for your children.

Chapter 4: How to Save Your Sanity. Spending an inordinate amount of time focused on the needs of your children combined with a lack of adult company can lead you to call into question your own sanity. In this chapter, you will discover practical tips and advice that you can implement every day that will help you to keep things in perspective and not become overwhelmed by your situation.

Chapter 5: Money, Money, Money. There's no escaping it, money makes the world go round. If you decide to not go back to your old job and the security of a regular salary, managing your money will rise even further up your priority list. In this chapter, we look at ways you can spend less and make the money you earn go further. We also explore ideas about how you can generate extra income while you are at home with your kids.

Chapter 6: Your Relationships. Becoming a mum has an impact on your relationship with everybody else in your life. In this chapter, we will look at your relationship with your partner, your parents and your friends, and how this may be impacted by becoming a mum and deciding to stay at home with your children.

Chapter 7: Your Confidence. Confidence is like a muscle: the more you use it, the stronger it gets. Your day-to-day life at home with your children may not allow you to be or to act as confidently as you once did. In this chapter, we look at some simple confidence-boosting techniques to help you maintain a positive outlook on life and yourself.

Chapter 8: Look After Yourself. As mums, our own well-being often drops down the family priority list. In this chapter, we discuss why this absolutely *must* not happen, why a 'happy mum' makes for a happy family and what you can do to commit to taking more time for *you*.

Chapter 9: Future-Proof Yourself. You may have decided that leaving your job behind to care for your children is your number one priority. However, one day, you may want or need to return to paid work. It's therefore paramount to 'future-proof' yourself. In this chapter, we look at some of the ways you can stay connected with the world of work and how to gain a different perspective on the skills you develop during the time that you spend away from the workplace.

Chapter 10: Start Your Own Business. For some women, it's impossible to reconcile the needs of family life and their own personal fulfilment. For that reason, they decide to take matters into their own hands and start a business. In this chapter, we look at some of the factors you need to consider about becoming self-employed, the types of self-employment available and how to decide which route is best for you.

Chapter 11: This Too Shall Pass. In this chapter, we take some time to reflect on how quickly time passes when your children are young and what to do if you don't enjoy being at home with your children.

By the end of the book, my hope for you is to feel reassured; reassured that staying at home with your children is a viable choice, reassured that you are not alone on this journey, because many brave women walk this path alongside you. And reassured that, no matter what other people say or think, the choices that you make will be the right ones for *you* and *your* family.

CHAPTER ONE

What's the Big Deal Anyway?

"Motherhood is tough. If you just want a wonderful little creature to love, you can get a puppy."

Barbara Walters

The transition to motherhood is an incredibly stressful period in any woman's life. I love this anecdote from Shannon Hyland-Tassava's book, *The Essential Stay-at-Home Mom Manual: How to have a Wondrous Life Amidst Kids and Chaos.*

"I figured out yesterday that between 7.30am and 10pm, I had a total of 25 minutes away from the incessant needs of one or the other baby, when I went outside for a very brief workout. You know – the nursing, the toddler not napping etc. Can you think of any other job where you work a 14-hour day with only 25 minutes of break time? And where you have to feed two other people during your lunch?

*And I'm not getting pay or retirement contributions
for this job because...?"*

The American Greeting Cards Store ran a fantastic advertising campaign for Mother's Day which showed a series of fake job interviews where the candidate was being interviewed for the role of Director of Operations. In the advert, the role was described to them like this:

> *"You will work 135 hours to unlimited hours per week. There are no breaks available. You can have lunch but only once the associate has finished their lunch. You must be able to work standing up most if not all of the time.*
>
> *There are no vacations. In fact, at holidays such as Thanksgiving, Christmas, New Years, the workload will go up and must be carried out with a happy disposition."*

I'm sure that you can relate to this scenario! One of the candidates responds to this list of demands with the retort: *"That's almost cruel".* You can watch the video here (http://youtu.be/4MLl60odCgY). If you were to look objectively at the workload involved in being a mum, you would agree with that applicant for the fake Director of Operations role – it's crazy. You can't possibly expect one person to do all that. But we do expect it. You do it. And millions of women take on that role and have done for thousands of years. We will continue to do so for many more thousands of years too.

Adjusting to life as a parent means dealing with sleep deprivation, constant worry about your child's well-being and endless decision-making, like breast vs bottle, sleep on back or tummy, send them to nursery to socialise or keep them at home with you, and so on. If, on top of becoming a mum, you also decide to leave the paid workforce, you have a double transition to contend with. In modern society, we place a high level of value on the job we do and the title we hold. When we no longer have that job title or fulfil that role, it can leave a gaping hole in our psyche. Often, it leads us to question who we are and what we're doing with our lives. You may even have started to question this yourself.

I've been at home with my kids for nearly six years now. During that time, I've had some interesting conversations with people, mainly older people, who have said things like, "You have children. You look after them and you get on with it. What's the big deal? What is so difficult about that?" To a certain extent, they're right. And yet, the world has changed dramatically since our grandparents' and parents' generations. Take a moment to reflect on this. How similar or different is your family setup to your own parents' or grandparents' experiences? Were you older or younger when you had your first child? Do you live closer to or further away from your immediate family? The changing landscape of our society has made the decision to give up your job and stay home with your children more difficult than ever.

Women have children when they're older

In 2014, the average age of new mothers hit 30 for the first time. When this statistic was revealed, the Office for National Statistics said, "The average age of mothers has been increasing since 1975, with increasing numbers of women delaying childbearing to later years." We now think nothing of a woman having her first child in her mid-to-late thirties. Yet when my mum had me in the late 1970s at the ripe old age of 38, she was considered a geriatric mother!

This trend towards having children later in life is down to a combination of factors. Some are very positive, such as the rising number of women engaged in higher education, the higher proportion of women who work and the prominence placed on women having a career. Some are not so positive, such as the rising cost of housing, and the increasing instability of partnerships and marriages.

One thing is for sure though: in general, women are having children later in life. This means they're spending longer periods of their life living BC (Before Children). Before entering the world of 'mumdom', they are building careers, travelling and enjoying their financial independence. What that means, of course, is that when the time comes to have a family and make the decision about whether to stay at home for their kids, there is a lot more to give up and a far bigger lifestyle adjustment to make.

We're more geographically dispersed

It used to be the norm that you were born in a particular town or village. You grew up there, settled there and had your children there – and the cycle continued. However, it's now increasingly common for people to move to different parts of the country, even across the globe. This change may be driven by their (or their partner's) job, or by a desire for adventure, and the urge to experience new places and different ways of life.

As a result, women who decide to stop working to look after their children are becoming more isolated. They are living further from where they grew up or from their family, so they don't have the practical and emotional support that can only come from their immediate family.

From a practical perspective, new mums who live a long way from their family have more limited childcare options, because geographically dispersed relations are not able to provide the level of support or help that is often needed. For some, this adds fuel to the fire of their desire to stay at home for their kids. The cost of childcare may be prohibitive, as is knowing there is no Plan B with relatives available to take care of sick children who may be unable to go to childcare some days.

In addition, the geographically dispersed family provides more challenges for mums. Traditionally, it was a woman's mother, grandmothers, aunts and sisters who would teach her the basic skills of looking after children, skills that she in turn would pass on to the younger members of her family. Now, new mums face a much lonelier existence and rely on the internet and books to teach them how to parent. Rather than being able to draw on the support of their family, mums need to be resourceful and build a support network for themselves.

On a recent visit, my mum commented on the number of social opportunities for mums and their children to meet up in my local area. She noted how different it was from when she was bringing up a family. And yes, there certainly are more family-friendly experiences available for mums (and dads) and their little ones than there was back in the day when my mum was raising four children, but she had a support network of grandparents, parents, aunts and uncles to rely on for moral support and entertainment.

The cost of living

The cost of living has rocketed in recent years and families increasingly *need* two incomes just to be able to put a roof over their heads and food on the table. The trend towards home-ownership and undertaking expensive mortgage commitments means that even families with a healthy income require two salaries in order to maintain their lifestyle.

This makes the decision for one parent to stay at home with the children harder still, to the point where being able to be a stay-at-home mum is considered a middle-class luxury rather than an option available to everyone.

Government policy

Encouraging mothers back into the workplace is a hot topic around the world. While these trends are global, my own experience centres on the UK environment for stay-at-home mums.

In recent years, in a bid to boost our stagnant economy and increase GDP, the UK Government has initiated a number of policies aimed at encouraging mothers out of the home and back into the workplace. The focus on helping mothers to become more economically active implies that women are valued more in terms of their economic worth and their financial contribution to the economy than as mothers. What these policies seems to overlook is the emotional and psychological contribution that stay-at-home mums make to society through nurturing and caring for their children.

The UK Government continually refers to mothers who have decided to stay at home with their children as women who have made a 'lifestyle choice'. This concept of a lifestyle choice does little to reflect the sacrifice that these women and their families make in order to enable one parent to be at home to look after the children.

All mainstream UK political parties are supportive of institutionalised childcare, expecting schools to take children at younger ages for longer school days and with shorter holiday periods. Apparently, it's important that we give our children the right foundation to their education, but little is said about making sure they get the right amount of nurturing, support and love – in other words, the kind of care they would get at home from their parents.

One result of this governmental attitude is that the value placed on the role of the carer has been diminished significantly. It's now the norm for us to hand over our children and have them looked after by professional care providers.

To further impact the stay-at-home choice, UK financial policy is heavily skewed in favour of dual-income families. In 2013, child benefit was withdrawn from families in which one or both parents are higher rate taxpayers (the income threshold being £42,475). Now, in times of austerity, this makes perfect sense. The Government has a limited pool of resources and cuts have to be made somewhere. However, in practice what this meant is that a single-income family earning £43,000 lost their child benefit while a dual-income family earning £84,950 (2 x £42,475) continued to receive child benefit. It doesn't seem fair, does it?

The current UK taxation system also fails to cater for families with a stay-at-home parent. A report released in 2011 by Care, a Christian social policy charity, called *The Taxation of Families 2009-10* contained a detailed assessment of the impact of the tax system on families compared with 33 other countries. It estimated that about 2.4 million children in Britain live in households where one parent is in full-time work and one is not working.

The report found that the tax burden had shifted markedly from single people without dependents to families. While the tax burden on most families and individuals was 'not out of line with that in other countries', it found that 'this is not the case with one-earner married couples with children'. British single-earner families with two children on £33,745 a year were paying 39% more in tax than comparable families from OECD countries. Quite an astonishing statistic, don't you think?

Campaign group Mothers at Home Matter (http://mothersathomematter.co.uk) works tirelessly to encourage the government to 'test' the impact of their policies on the affordability and quality of family life. I would highly recommend looking at their website if you're interested in this issue.

So what does that mean for us?

In short, staying at home with the kids is no longer the norm. In 1981, only 24% of women returned to work within a year of giving birth; by 2001, that number had risen to 67%. In 2010, the Department for Work and Pensions reported that 76% of mothers returned to work within 12 to 18 months of having a child. Returning to work after maternity leave is now what the majority of society expects mums to do.

Given this modern social landscape where work is so highly valued, it's easy to see that any mum making the decision about staying at home to look after her children faces an immense amount of pressure to return to paid work.

Our society has changed massively in recent years. The family norm now is for two parents to work and the children to be looked after outside the home. This means the decision about whether to stay at home and raise your own children has become much more complex than ever before.

The great news is help is at hand to support you making your decision. The prospect of making this decision may seem gloomy at first glance, but I'm here to help you see how the stay-at-home option could be workable. Let's weigh up the options.

CHAPTER TWO

The Decision to Stay at Home

"When your values are clear to you, making decisions becomes easier."

Roy E. Disney

The decision about returning to work after maternity leave is unique and personal to each individual family. If you're at the point of making this decision, I'd like to offer some food for thought to help you choose the best path for you and your family.

For some women, the decision about whether to stay at home or return to work is very clear-cut. The majority, though, probably sit in a grey area in the middle. They look at the precious little person they've brought into the world and feel sick at the thought of leaving them… Equally, they can feel daunted at the thought of staying at home with a small child all day. They wonder if they're cut out to be a stay-at-home mum at all. Some women consider starting a home-based business while caring for their children, but then worry about having what it takes to succeed. They wonder if they should just return to 'normality' where they'll have the opportunity to 'use their brain' and get a guaranteed salary at the end of the month.

For those who are stranded in that grey zone, the decision about whether to return to work after maternity leave can be a tortuous process. Your priorities shift dramatically with the arrival of your child and this results in a lot of conflicting emotions and thoughts. On the one hand, it seems absolutely impossible to hand over your child to be cared for by somebody else so you can return to work; on the other hand, it seems utterly preposterous that you should sign yourself up for caring for a little person 24/7 with no financial reward and little opportunity to get out into the 'real world'.

> *"Follow your heart. Every decision involves loss. The decision to stay home involves the loss of that 'other' life and possibly the substantial loss of income. The decision to work outside of the home involves separation and loss for you and your children.*
>
> *There is no 'having it all'. There is no getting away without loss. So focus on the gain. What fills your heart with most joy? Go with it. Your decision lies there."*
>
> Stay-at-home mum of two

The decision to return to work is one you will need to make with your heart *and* your head. Although the heart will play a major part in your decision to stay at home, the head needs first to take care of a few matters...

Can you afford to stop working?

Let's face it. This is the crux, isn't it? Can you afford to stay at home with your little ones or not? The answer to this question is pretty fundamental to your decision-making process. How much money do you need to be able to survive as a family? And can your family still earn that amount of money if you don't return to your old job?

"When I handed in my resignation letter, I was absolutely terrified! I knew I wanted to be at home with my daughter and that my husband earned enough to pay the bills, but I also knew we would need to live on a tight budget. I wasn't sure how I would cope without my 'treats' and my shoe fund!"

Megan, stay at home mum of two

When thinking about your finances, it's useful to divide the money that you need into two categories: first, the money you need to meet your basic needs; and second, the money you need for your longer-term plans.

Meeting your basic needs

This is the first and most fundamental issue that you need to consider when you're thinking about giving up your job after maternity leave. Quite simply, if you don't go back to work, can you still afford to keep a roof over your head and put food on the table? I'm not necessarily referring to the roof that you currently have or the food that you put on the table right now. I'm talking about an acceptable roof and acceptable food. If you lose your salary from the family budget, will you be able to pay for a place to live, food to eat and your normal day-to-day bills?

On top of these basic financial requirements, it's worth factoring in a small financial cushion in case something happens and you need some emergency money. Having a small amount of savings will give you the confidence to know that you will be able to deal with unexpected events like a broken boiler or a car that won't start.

Longer-term financial plans

In addition to ensuring you have enough income to meet your basic needs, you may also want to think about what your financial plans are for the next five to ten years. In particular, what will be the impact of not returning to work on what you're able to do? Let me give you an example. Think about whether you are planning to move house. If you leave your job, how will that impact your ability to get a mortgage in the future? If you decide to take some time off to care for your family, how will that impact your pension plans or long-term savings? Is this something you're comfortable with?

You would expect the time when you have only one income to be a lean period for your family finances. This is perfectly acceptable, but it is worth looking ahead to how you can make up any shortfall in later years.

> *"We had to make some tough decisions. We desperately wanted to move out of our flat and have a house with a garden, but at the same time we really wanted to give James the security of having me at home to look after him. It was disappointing to put off our plans to move to a bigger place, but I know we won't regret our decision."*
>
> Vicky, stay-at-home mum of one

How much will you earn if you return to work?

Working out exactly how much better off you would be if you return to work is a minefield. Make sure that you realistically account for the cost of childcare, travel, clothes, lunches etc when you're working out how much you will take home each month. Factor in any commitment you have to repay your maternity allowance if you do not return to your old job and make sure you know exactly how much money you will have left over each month after you've paid all of your expenses. This will allow you to weigh up the impact that your salary will have on your household budget in a more realistic way.

> *"When I was on maternity leave, my job specification changed and my pay scale reduced. Everybody holding that role was made redundant*

and offered re-employment in the new role. I worked out that (provided I took a packed lunch and fuel prices didn't rise), after childcare expenses, I would be working for £25 a month and would only see my child for bath and bed (teething and traffic permitting) during the week."

Stay-at-home mum of one

Also try to work out whether your family is entitled to any financial support from the government and factor this into your budget. For example, will your income be higher if you work three days a week rather than four, because you will pay less tax? Will working fewer hours mean you're entitled to benefits that you wouldn't be eligible for if you worked more hours? Make sure you know all the facts before making any decisions about returning to work.

Let's talk about benefits

The benefits available to families with young children vary from country to country around the world. It's well worth investigating the support available in your country and what you're entitled to claim.

In the UK, there is a real stigma attached to receiving benefits. However, if you've been a working member of society, paying taxes and making your contribution up until the time your children come along, there's absolutely nothing wrong with identifying how the state can support your family once you have children. There's no reason why you'll need to have this support in the long term. But if staying at home with your children is important to you and state benefits would help you to do that, make sure you're taking advantage of your entitlements.

Making sensible financial decisions

Once you look at your family's finances objectively, you'll be in a better position to decide what options are available to you. Perhaps you need to work a minimum of three days a week to make sure your family can cover the bills, but find that once you factor in the cost of childcare it's only financially viable for you to work four or more days a week. Perhaps it doesn't make financial sense for you to return to work at all. The decision will depend on your personal circumstances.

Once you have made all of your calculations, you might realise that you can't afford to maintain your basic standard of living unless you go back to work. If you find yourself unable to cover your standard monthly outgoings from your partner's salary or from some other source of income, then you have some serious thinking to do. Sadly, money does indeed make the world go round. Or at least, it provides us with the ability to have a place to live and food to eat. You will either need to go back to your old job or find the same income from elsewhere and be confident that you'll be able to find this money on a consistent basis.

If you do think that your family could survive financially without your income, there are some other 'heart-related' factors to take into consideration when deciding whether to leave work behind and stay home for the kids.

What type of mum do you want to be?

From the outset, I want you to discover and keep front of mind the type of mum you want to be.

I always ask the mums I work with to take some time to think about their mum style. To figure this out, I encourage them to do something that makes them feel very uncomfortable: write their own eulogy.

Now, I know that might feel a bit (or a lot!) strange, but writing your own eulogy is a very common exercise used in life and business coaching. You may have already been asked to do this at school, college or university, or even on a course at work. Rest assured this exercise is often met with a degree of trepidation, so you're not alone if you feel a little daunted. It is, however, a proven tool to help us all answer the question: how do I want people to remember me?

The objective of this exercise is to help people understand the type of person they aspire to be and then take a good look at their own life to understand how closely they currently live in line with this ideal. To tailor this exercise to our purposes as mums or mums-to-be, I suggest looking at the question from a slightly different perspective here and ask yourself: how do I want my children to remember me? When it gets to that day (hopefully a long, long time from now) when your children are looking back on your life, what type of memories do you want them to have of you as a parent and of their childhood? What do they remember about family life when they were growing up? What type of parent were you?

When you're clear about the type of parent you want to be, so many other aspects of your life slot into place. I believe that and I've experienced it for myself. For example, I have huge ambitions for my business. I would love to support mums all over the world to develop a business that works around their family. I have a million ideas a day about products I could create and programmes I could run to make a difference and help other mums. But doing that would require a massive investment of my time. My children are still very young and I have a clear view of the type of mum I want to be. That involves being around for them as much as possible. That means my business will just have to grow a bit more slowly to begin with. I have no doubt that I will get to support mums all over the world; it's just a question of timing!

I can envisage what I'd like my kids to say at my funeral. And because of that, I've decided to scale back my ambitions– for now. When they're older, I'll be able to devote more time to my business. For now though, I'm going to enjoy building it gradually.

Just to reiterate, I know that answering the question about what you want your kids to say about you once you're gone is uncomfortable, but please give it a go. It will give you a real sense of clarity about what is important to you.

At my funeral (a long, long time from today) I want (insert the name of your children) to say that I (insert your name) was_____.

What kind of childhood did you have?

The type of childhood you had will influence your decision about how to raise your own family. You may have happy memories of after-school picnics with your mum and your siblings or you may remember a deeply embarrassing time when your teenage friends teased you that your mum was 'just a mum'. What bits of your childhood would you replicate for your own children and which things would you like to do differently from your parents?

"Some friends talk about being proud of their working mums making strides in the corporate world when it was more uncommon then. For me, I remember that my mum was always in the house when I got home from school – ready with a biscuit and to listen about my day.

That five to ten minutes of downloading the day with her was so important to me and my emotional health. I just couldn't imagine not doing the same for my children."

Nicola Dawes, mum of two,
founder of Stripey Stork

Time is priceless

*"Time is free, but it's priceless. You can't own
it, but you can use it. You can't keep it, but you
can spend it. Once you've lost it, you can never
get it back."*

Harvey Mackay

This probably looks like the kind of quote that you've seen
floating around your Facebook page trying to inspire you
to make more of your life. You probably gave it a quick
glance and then moved on to a status update about your
ex-colleague's daughter's ear infection. But here's the
thing. Time is our most valuable commodity. We can have
all the 'stuff' in the world, but if we don't have time to
enjoy and value it then we have nothing.

Every year for sixteen years in the run up to Mother's Day,
Erin Kurt, a teacher from the USA, would ask her students
to tell her what they loved to do with their parents. Each
student was asked to think about what their mother or
guardian did for or with them that made them feel happy
or loved. From what they told her, Erin Kurt compiled a
list of the top things children love to do with their parents:
(http://www.lifehack.org/articles/lifestyle/the-top-10-
things-children-really-want-their-parents-to-do-with-
them.html).

Here is a list of the top ten things students around the
world said they remembered and loved most about their
mothers.

1. Come into my bedroom at night, tuck me in and sing me a song. Also she would tell me stories about when I was little.

2. Give me hugs and kisses and sit and talk with me privately.

3. Spend quality time just with me when my brothers and sisters were not around.

4. Give me nutritious food so I could grow up healthy.

5. Talk to me at dinner about what we could do together on the weekend.

6. Talk to me at night about anything: love, school, family etc.

7. Let me play outside a lot.

8. Cuddle under a blanket and watch our favourite TV shows together.

9. Discipline me. It made me feel like she cared.

10. Leave special messages in my desk or lunch bag.

What our children really want is our time and attention. No doubt, they would love to have the latest Disney doll that sings when you press a button or a special Christmas outing to the theatre. When it comes down to it, though, all our children wish for is to feel safe and loved, and spend time with their parents.

You only get one shot

"You only get one shot, do not miss your chance to blow,
This opportunity comes once in a lifetime, yo."

Lose Yourself, Eminem

Having your first child, you tend to get lots of well-meaning (and probably older) friends and relatives tell you that you should treasure every minute with your little one as he or she will grow up fast. Well, let me tell you, I was in no mood to treasure every minute when I was bouncing up and down on a birthing ball trying to soothe a screaming, colicky newborn. I thought I was going to go silently insane with this new, slower (much slower) pace of life.

I also felt completely trapped as I was restricted to within a two-mile radius of my home. Super Girl hated the car and wasn't wild about public transport either. We spent much of those first few months at home or travelling on foot. But I slowly adjusted to this slightly strange new life where (for the first time ever) I was doing something that I felt was truly important, worthwhile and useful. Yet there was nobody to reward me with a pay cheque at the end of each month or a performance review at the end of each year telling me what a good job I was doing. And, as the months ticked on and Super Girl became more mobile and vocal, I realised that those well-meaning friends and relatives were right.

Our little ones grow up fast – really, really fast. One minute Super Girl was lying helplessly in my arms unable to support her own head. Then in the blink of an eye, she was a little person with an opinion who was throwing my lovingly made roasted vegetable chips on the floor and demanding 'more puffs'. (You know those hideous orange posh Wotsits that we kid ourselves are okay to give our kids because they're organic and carrot-flavoured?)

I think I'm pretty fortunate to have appreciated this very early on in her life. I like to think of myself as a multi-skilled and talented person; there are many things I could be doing with my time. However, there is only one job that *only* I can do and that's be a mum to Super Girl and Boy Wonder. You only get one shot at this parenthood lark: you only get one shot at being there when your little people are truly little. You only get one shot at helping your school-age children to read and write, to navigate the world and learn right from wrong. You only get one shot at supporting your teenager through the angst and trauma of friendships that have gone wrong, and the stress of exams and university applications.

"It's hard, but wonderful. Be aware of what you're letting yourself in for. The days can be relentlessly long, but the years are short. Don't miss them."

Charlotte, stay-at-home mum of one

I'm not by any means saying that you need to be defined solely by your children and that your entire life should be devoted to them at the expense of your own dreams, ambitions and desires. I'm saying that you only get one shot at being a parent. Make sure, whatever you choose to do with that one shot, it's exactly how you want it to be.

Damned if you do and damned if you don't!

I'm sure, as part of making your decision, you've done some research about whether it's better for your kids if you stay at home or they're looked after by a childcare provider, like a nursery, childminder or nanny. There's a wealth of conflicting evidence out there.

Some of the research advocates staying at home with your children because it is the best thing you can do for your child's emotional health, well-being and development. According to psychologist Oliver James, children are damaged emotionally and psychologically by being put into childcare at a young age.

> *"A responsive mother who is there for the child in the early years is the best possible carer... Studies show that daycare is less good for under-threes than childminders, who are less good than nannies, who are less good than close relatives, who are less good than parents."*

> Oliver James

Conversely, other research indicates that young children who are immersed in a nursery setting show no ill-effects from it. A 2009 study by Family Children Childcare followed 1,000 babies from the age of three months to three years and found there was no connection between the amount of childcare experienced by a baby and behavioural problems when they reached 36 months.

Personally, I think you should take any research with a pinch of salt. Ultimately, only you and your partner can decide what is right for your family. Research is all well and good, but it covers such a wide section of the population that it's almost impossible to predict whether the recommendations made will apply to your specific situation. You know your family, you know your children, and you know what's going to work best for you personally.

Staying home with the kids does not automatically guarantee that your children will grow up to be happy, well-adjusted, socially confident individuals. But it does give you the reassurance that you have done what you think is the right thing and given your child the family life that you want them to have.

What will people think?

Being a parent is the most public job that you will ever do. By that, I mean that it is a job that you do openly in front of family, friends and the general public. Whether you like it or not, your performance as a parent is visible to everybody around you. If you have an off-day at work, you can keep a low profile. Sadly, when it comes to parenting, there is nowhere to run and nowhere to hide. And you can bet your bottom dollar that everybody observing your parenting skills has an opinion on how well you're doing your job!

When you decide to stay home with the kids, everyone you know will have a view on what you are doing. You've got to remember that they are all looking at the situation from very different perspectives.

> *"It does sometimes drive me mad when other mums (my sister included!) say to me 'I couldn't do what you do' [staying at home]. I'm never quite sure what that means!"*
>
> Kate, stay-at-home mum of two

Your own mother might have continued to work all the way through your childhood and be surprised by your decision. The friends you've known all through your education and career might be horrified that you are now 'throwing it all away'. Your siblings might be slightly bemused that their quick-tempered, stroppy little sister is **actually** intending to spend the majority of her day looking after young children. That nice lady that works at the pharmacy might be pleased you've decided to stay at home with the kids because 'in her day that's what everybody did'.

Everyone will have an opinion about your decision.

Everyone! Some will be positive; some not so positive. Certain people will be open and talk to you about it; others will keep their thoughts to themselves. All you need to do throughout this time is be strong and have confidence in the decision you've made. It really doesn't matter what anyone else thinks. I know it can be tough to manage, but all that counts is what's right for your family according to you.

> *"It drives me crazy when other people judge my decision: 'Aren't you bored? When are you going to get a real job again? Don't you feel you've lost your identity? Don't you need me-time?'*
>
> *Of course, my children drive me crazy. They strop, flounce, tantrum, are stubborn, fiercely independent, messy and don't even get me started on mealtimes or teeth-cleaning, but I made an active decision to take this path.*
>
> *I don't expect other people to make their life choices based on my situation and I hate it that I am often judged for wanting to stay at home and look after my family. I tried, and failed, to balance my old job and my family. I had to make a choice and I chose to stay at home with my kids"*
>
> Karen, stay-at-home mum of two

Your decision to stay at home with your kids may be the talk of the town, or the family gathering, or the staff room... or wherever! Just know it will be a five-minute wonder. Everybody will very quickly move onto someone else's life and someone else's decisions.

"There have been sentiments voiced such as, 'It's alright for you. You can afford to.' (We couldn't really at first but we cut back.) And, 'You're wasting all your education and career being stuck at home'.

It's not the common thing to stay at home now so there's always a curiosity about it and a need for me to try to justify why I've chosen to do so.

Other women are always keen to tell me how their kids are thriving at nursery, and how great it is to get a break away from them while they're at work, and how the extra money is handy for holidays etc – as if, if they point it out to me, I'll realise where I've gone wrong and see the light."

Harper, stay-at-home mum of two

Let's stop the judgements

Reports about 'mummy wars' exhaust me: the working parents who call the stay-at-home mums lazy, the stay-at-home mums who chastise the working mums for abandoning their children to childcare… I have to be honest. I'm not convinced the 'mummy wars' even exist. Or at least not to the extent the press would have us believe.

Do we really, day to day, as mums, have that much time

left to cast judgement over the other mums around us? We are all so busy getting on with our lives - I'm pretty sure we don't! I do think, however, that there's a large proportion of the media that uses these so-called mummy wars as a way to stir up a reaction amongst their readers and viewers.

If you have decided to stay at home and are feeling even the tiniest bit judgemental of the women you know who have decided to go back to paid work, I would urge you to stop. It's just not worth it. You've made the decision that's right for *your* family. You will have your reasons why you passionately believe that you should be at home with your family. The same applies for the women who have returned to work, too. They have made a decision based on what they believe to be right for their family. Let them get on with it! Whether you approve or disapprove makes absolutely no difference. And before you say, "Ah but it's not me, I'm fine with women returning to work. It's them who look down on me because I've decided to stay at home", forget it. Even if a small minority think that way, stop, because it's not a valuable use of your time or energy even entertaining that thought.

The decision is entirely yours

Throughout your maternity leave, the conversation with other mums will be littered with discussions about returning to work and finding appropriate childcare.

Since you're considering staying at home with your kids – or have already made the decision – you may be feeling like you're in the minority.

As we've seen, though, it's a decision that you and your partner need to make for your family. Nobody else can make the decision for you. You need to do what is right for your specific situation, because other people don't know all the factors: your finances, your job role, your upbringing, your desires. It's all about you. And for some women, there may even come a defining moment that tips the scales in a particular direction.

liked to eat because she didn't know. I didn't want to have that kind of relationship with my children."

Amy, stay-at-home mum of one

For other mums, this is a decision that needs to be made over a longer period of time and with an eye to the implications for the future. Whenever and however you make the decision, as long as it's your choice, taking into account all the factors we've covered here, it will be the right one for you and your family.

CHAPTER THREE

The Reality of Being Home with the Kids

*"If there were no schools to take the children
away from home part of the time, the insane
asylums would be filled by mothers."*

Edgar W Hove

When you ask anybody who has decided to stay at home with their kids what gives them 'job satisfaction' as a parent, the answer almost always involves 'being there for the milestones'. Yes, it is wonderful to be there for the first word, the first steps... the first time they manage to spoon the majority of a bowl of porridge into their hungry little mouth without tipping it all over the floor. And yes, of course, all these achievements by your child gives you a sense of pride and satisfaction as a parent. Hasn't your little person done well? Aren't they so clever? Aren't we so lucky to have been there to witness it?

It's not all about the milestones

The truth is that being at home with the kids is not just about being there for the milestones. After the first step come the next million steps that we can be around to see. After that first word, there will be many more words, sentences, conversations. It evolves. Being at home with the kids is about being there for all of it - the good, the bad and the downright ugly. The saying goes that we 'hurt the people we love the most'. Well, if that is true, then my children love me very, very much. I bet your kids are the same!

When I look back on my life and think about my stand-out moments, I probably won't count the time that Boy Wonder was teething and bit me on the thigh so hard that he drew blood. I probably won't be rushing to remember the time (or if I'm honest, the many, many times) that Super Girl sobbed uncontrollably because she didn't want a bath and had to be left alone crying naked at the bottom of the stairs because if you went any closer she would become hysterical. I am sure that your kids have 'treated' you to similar events!

When we sign up to staying at home with our children, we think about the glorious milestones that we get to witness. Yet, these other far less glamorous events are the moments along the journey that make the difference. These are the moments when our children truly need us around. These are the moments that they learn about life. These are the moments that are important. These are the moments that our children need and want us there. It's how we handle every one of these moments that will shape the people they become.

Growing up can be a bumpy ride. Our children need to learn how to navigate the world and work out what's an acceptable way to behave and what isn't. That's when they must have that trusted person around to keep them on the straight and narrow. As a mum, it's hugely rewarding to be there for the good bits, but as a child, it means the world to have your mum around for the bad bits too.

You need to slow down

We all tend to live life at breakneck speed these days, but when we spend time with young children, we have to make a huge adjustment and slow down so we live life at their pace. When Super Girl was a newborn, we would be up, dressed, fed, the house tidied and at least one circuit of the local park completed by 9.30am. I was then left wondering what I was supposed to do with the rest of the day. That gave us a lot of time to do not very much; at that time, I found this hugely frustrating. As she got older and I started to relax and not feel the need to constantly 'do', that amount of activity would keep us occupied for at least half a day.

"My days have a slower pace, and I truly appreciate and enjoy the simple, smaller things, like nature and

the changing seasons as I have time to. As a high-achieving ex-City lawyer, it was startling to realise, as arrogant as it sounds, that I can choose to not do everything and that being organised does not translate to being a happy mother. Children don't run to timetables and sometimes not everything is in your control (in fact, life rarely is) and this was an eye-opener!"

Stay-at-home mum of one

If you've ever taken a toddler for a walk, you will know that they are incapable of getting anywhere quickly. There are piles of leaves to explore, spider webs to admire and police cars to watch. We could probably learn a thing or two from our toddlers. We're often so busy racing around trying to do and achieve more that we forget to stop and look and truly appreciate what is happening around us. As you spend more time at home with the kids, you may start to relax into this slower way of life.

"I have realised I enjoy fairly simple pleasures and life isn't about grabbing a Starbucks coffee on the way into work, having multiple pairs of shoes and being wined and dined by my media suppliers any more.

It's much simpler than that.

The warmth of sun on your face, the sound of the breeze in the trees and the laughter of toddlers playing in the meadow.

This might sound fanciful and, of course, the daily grind is always there no matter what you do. But I feel more connected and in control of what I really want to do.

There is pleasure and a sense of achievement in what I do, every day."

Sarah Sproston, mum of two
and owner of Aunty Sarah Childminding

The wonderful poet and blogger Rebekah Knight summed up this need to slow down in her poem 'Slow Down Mummy':

"slow down mummy, there is no need to rush,
slow down mummy, what is all the fuss?
slow down mummy, make yourself a cup of tea.
slow down mummy, come spend some time
with me.

slow down mummy, let's pull boots on for a
walk,
let's kick at piles of leaves, and smile and laugh
and talk.
slow down mummy, you look ever so tired,
come sit and snuggle under the duvet, and rest
with me a while.

slow down mummy, those dirty dishes can
wait,
slow down mummy, let's have some fun - bake
a cake!

slow down mummy, I know you work a lot,
but sometimes mummy, it's nice when you just
stop.

sit with us a minute,
and listen to our day,
spend a cherished moment,
because our childhood won't stay!"

It's not just about the early years

My children are still young and very much physically, mentally and emotionally dependent on me on a daily basis. I have been told by the parents of older children that, as the years go on, while the physical dependence lessens and our children are able to dress and care for themselves, they can still be as emotionally and mentally dependent on their parents.

The teenage years in particular are a tricky time for our children. They have to learn how to navigate the grown-up world. They are forming their own opinions and can be even more heavily influenced by their peers. They are expected to make difficult life choices about their education and their future at a relatively young age. Again, in the past we may have called upon other family members to act as a support and guide in these situations, but this is often no longer possible due to the modern-day geographically dispersed family.

Depending on the issues that arise in your family, being

around for your teenage children may be just as important as being around for them when they were little, if not more.

Nobody appreciates you

To say 'nobody appreciates you' is probably a gross exaggeration, but with the exception of other stay-at-home mums, very few people will appreciate the amount of time, work and effort that you put into your family.

When you think about a GP working in a busy surgery, filling their day with patient appointments, you can appreciate the amount of effort they've put in. They've had to draw on their training and expertise to diagnose patients, wrestle with admin, be sensitive to the needs of their patients, treating them sympathetically and with respect. They have worked hard.

When you think about a cleaner in an office block, always on their feet, employed in manual labour that is often backbreaking work, you can appreciate the amount of effort they've put in. They have been tidying and cleaning, often completing their work while trying not to disturb others. They have worked hard.

Then you have a stay-at-home mum. She's been at home all day playing with her children… or at least that's what you may think if you aren't a parent and have never spent much time with children. Those who don't spend a lot of time with children often fail to recognise the multiple roles that a stay-at-home mum takes on, sometimes simultaneously.

The website mom.salary.com estimates that in 2014 a stay-at-home mum juggled 96.5 hours of work each week. If these women had been paid for their role of facilities manager, housekeeper, nursery teacher, chauffeur (and countless other roles), they would have earned $118,905, based on the average earnings for these roles. These types of surveys are quite fun to look at but, coming back down to reality with a bump, motherhood does not come with a salary attached to it. (Let alone a six-figure salary!)

You can either get annoyed about this or you can accept it. In reality, unless someone has walked in your shoes, they can never fully appreciate the work that you do as a mother or the value that you bring to your children and your family. It is much more important to have confidence in yourself and know that what you're doing is of value for your family than to look for appreciation from others.

You're not a housekeeper

There is a common misconception that because you are at home with the kids that your house should be spotlessly clean and perfectly organised at all times. You are, after all, at home all day so how is it possible that you are not on top of the washing and have your floors mopped and gleaming? Erm… because you are at home all day with children!

If you're at home then you're going to make a mess. If the entire household gets up, dressed and goes out in the morning then the house will lie empty all day and there is nobody around to mess it up.

Unless you want to devote 24 hours a day to having the perfect home, then you will have to accept that your house will only ever get to a standard that is 'good enough'. You just need to work out what good enough means to you! You didn't give up your job to become a housekeeper. You gave up your job to look after your children. The two are completely separate things. Of course, one part of looking after your children means giving them a safe, warm environment to grow up in but that doesn't mean that you have to permanently don your marigolds and scrub the floors.

"Good mums have sticky floors, dirty ovens and happy kids"

Unknown

When you're at home with the kids, there's a temptation to get caught up in a never-ending loop of domestic jobs. Very rarely will you have a sense of satisfaction of a job well done because you can guarantee that just as you finish something, someone – probably a little person – is going to come along and mess it up.

Last night, I decided to hoover the downstairs of the house. This task usually takes me about three times longer than it should because Boy Wonder and Super Girl like to pretend the hoover is a monster that they must escape from. Once he is feeling brave enough, Boy Wonder rugby tackles the hoover (while I am still using it) so that he can slay the beast and protect his sister. Last night, when the vacuuming was done, I put the hoover away only to come back 30 seconds later to find that he had found a little Tupperware box of cereal underneath his pushchair. He had opened it up and spilled it, crumbs and all, on the living room carpet. I give up! Trying to keep a house tidy with young children around is like brushing your teeth while eating chocolate. Pointless!

That doesn't mean that you can just ignore housework altogether (which is a pity!) but it does mean that you need to define your own 'good enough', your own endpoint, so that you know when to call time on it. You probably don't want spend your entire day doing the same task over and over again. More on this in Chapter Four: How to Save Your Sanity.

Your work will never be done

I often watch with envy as my husband goes off to work in the morning. He works very hard, often very long hours, but one thing he can be sure of is that each project he works on has a beginning, a middle and an end. There may be obstacles along the way that don't let him complete his work as quickly as he would like, but he knows that at some point he will get on track and finish what he started.

"Initially, the biggest challenge of being at home was realising that, unlike in the work environment with projects and tasks to achieve within deadlines, being a mum is a constant project with numerous dependent tasks that all need to be managed in the moment. No timeline to work to, just tasks that need to be done now. Coming to terms with the fact that on some days you achieved few or none of those tasks was a big challenge to accept."

Katie, stay-at-home mum of one

When you're home with kids, your work rarely has a beginning, a middle and an end. Let's look at the average day in your kitchen: you get up in the morning, prepare breakfast, half of it gets eaten, half of it ends up on the floor. After breakfast, you start to tidy up but you get distracted by a dirty nappy. You finally manage to get the breakfast dishes washed and you start to put them away, but then your eldest child comes looking for a snack. You give him a bag of mini rice cakes and he drops a few on the floor but it's fine because you've still not cleared up the cereal from breakfast. You get the brush out to sweep it up but your youngest appears and wants to 'help'. Finally, you manage to sweep all of the leftover food and crumbs into a pile and you go to get the dustpan and brush, but when you turn around you find that your youngest has 'helped' by spreading all of the debris back around the kitchen.

While you've been doing this your eldest has taken all of

the plastic cups out of the cupboard and started to build a tower with them and is now asking if he can play with water… Your kitchen is still not tidy, but it's 9.30am and if you don't leave now you'll be late for toddler group. You can sort out the kitchen when you get back.

I'm sure this scenario is very familiar to you! And you know that when you get back from toddler group you are never going to get that kitchen 'sorted' the way that you'd like to.

"The unrelenting boredom and repetition of domestic chores is soul-destroying! Yet another load of washing... Not broken up by any more stimulating activity, it can be such a grind"

Helen, mum of two,
co-owner of Busy Lizzy, Reigate

Being at home with children means contending with an endless cycle of tasks that never truly get finished. The laundry basket will be empty for half a day before it starts filling up again. Little tummies will be full for a couple of hours before they need more food to keep them going. Floors, bathrooms and surfaces will be clean for five minutes before they start to get dirty again. That's life. As the person who never gets to finish her work, it's easy to get frustrated but you've got to remember that the cogs need to keep turning. This is the perfectly normal and natural rhythm of family life and you are doing the best that you can to keep it all moving in the right direction.

Oh, the monotony!

Children love routine; children thrive on routine. They love to have a set pattern of events to guide their day and to help them feel secure. They like to know exactly what is coming next and what is expected of them. Mums, on the other hand, sometimes love this routine a little less. Having the same pattern to every day can become tedious. Some days can feel like an endless round of meal preparation, tidying up, walking to the same shops to buy the same things, laundry, bath time and getting children to sleep.

Even the fun bits of being a mum can get monotonous after a while. How many more times can you recite the story of the moment? (You can already do it in your sleep!) How many more times do you have to pick up the rattle from the floor? (It has already been propelled from the high chair at least a hundred times today!) How much longer can you keep building a tower and knocking it down? (You've been doing it for 45 minutes already!)

Being at home with the kids can be incredibly monotonous at times. As your children get that little bit older, the constraints of being a stay-at-home mum change because your day ends up revolving around dropping them off at school or pre-school and picking them up at again. All the ferrying around means you become quite geographically constrained as there's only so far you can go and only so much you can do in the time between dropping them off and picking them up.

But what we see as monotony and boring repetition, our children see as safety and security. They know how the day is going to pan out. They know what is expected of them. Doing the same things over and over again is how they learn. Reading the same stories countless times is how they will eventually start to recognise the shapes of letters, identify different colours and see patterns in things. Helping them to draw a smiley face over and over again is how they will learn how to hold a pencil – and eventually make marks that are meaningful to other people and not just to themselves. Getting a 'mummy hug' for the twentieth time in an hour is how they know that they are safe, secure and loved. The monotony can be frustrating, but there is a purpose to it. All of these small repetitions build solid foundations for our children.

You will never experience this amount of love again

So far I've probably not painted a very favourable picture of being at home with the kids. At times, it's tiring, frustrating and monotonous, but there are some very real upsides to it as well.

Your children love you more than anybody else in the whole wide world. The bond between parent and child is one of the strongest connections in nature. You love and fiercely protect your children and in return your children love and feel safe with you. When you are at home with your children, you get to experience this love on a daily basis: the kisses, the cuddles, the hours of snuggling in beside you, following you around the house and just wanting to be close to you.

If you find this level of affection claustrophobic or overwhelming, remind yourself that it won't last forever. In the blink of an eye, your little people will become big people and may be too embarrassed to show the love that they feel for you. The love itself won't go away, they will just be 'too cool' to express it. Your children won't love you any more or any less because you have chosen to stay at home with them rather than going out to work, but if you decide to stay at home you will get to experience their love and affection more often.

"Being a mum, you have constant motivation to do better and be a better person as a role model for your children.

At work, I could be stressed for a whole day and take that stress home at night. At home, I am stressed for half an hour then have a hug or watch them looking beautiful and peaceful having a nap and feel better.

At the end of the day when he says, 'I've had a lovely day, Mummy' even when I have told him 'no' a hundred times, my heart melts and I am ready for anything."

Stay-at-home mum of one

You've never had more freedom – or more constraints

When you are at home with young children you will probably have more freedom than you have had at almost any other point in your life, although it may not feel like it at the time. If you are used to working set hours and only having a certain number of days' holiday a year, then being at home with your children can feel incredibly liberating. You don't have to be anywhere at a particular time, you can take holidays when you want to and be the master of your own destiny.

This changes when your children get a little older and you become constrained by school hours and school holidays, but when your children are young, you can enjoy this moment of freedom. It is a luxury that I think is very easy to overlook. You can spend time in parks when they are virtually empty, go for impromptu picnics when the weather is fine, jump in those big piles of leaves when they are really crisp and right at their leaf-jumping best.

Now along with freedom come some fairly major constraints as well. You are now responsible for looking after another human, maybe a few. Each of them has a mind of his or her own and might not always be in the mood to do what you want to do. Every single thing that you do each day has to accommodate a little person. If you go on a train journey, you need to plan out how you get the pushchair up and down the stairs at the station. If you go to the supermarket, you need to find a trolley that holds the baby's car seat. The trick is to make the most of your freedom and not get too bogged down by the constraints. Identify the places that you want to go and the things that you want to do and just go for it. Sure, you'll have some disastrous days out but you'll also have some great adventures as well.

"I remember being incredibly excited about taking Thomas to Birmingham for the first time. Me and my boy in the Big City on our own. I had the entire journey planned out in meticulous detail. I even drove to a train station three miles away so that I would have step-free access. I had researched child-friendly places to feed and change him. It was so exciting and so daunting at the same time."

Susie, stay-at-home mum of one

There is the extraordinary in the ordinary

Everyday life is pretty ordinary. When you share everyday life with children, though, it can become extraordinary. Before, in the workplace, one cold November morning heading to the office was probably much the same as any other. You probably rushed out of the door, jumped in the car or ran to the train station and just went to work. When you're at home with the children, a cold November morning involves corralling little people into snuggly, warm clothes, heading out the door and admiring the hundreds of spider webs that have appeared overnight. A spider web – it's something so simple that you probably just hurried past before now. With your children, it takes on a whole new magical quality. Where have the spiders gone? Why did they decide to make their web in that particular place? Look at how the dewdrops make the spider webs sparkle and glisten in the sun? How can we cross through over the path without breaking the spider web?

Who would have thought that so much entertainment and happiness could come from spider webs? Seeing the world through the eyes of children can change your perspective drastically. It gives you the opportunity to see the world in a different light and appreciate everything around you. You start to see the extraordinary in the ordinary...

> *"If I could see the world through the eyes of a child, what a wonderful world this would be. There'd be no trouble and no strife, just a happy life with a bluebird in every tree."*
>
> *If I Could See the World*, Patsy Cline

When you think about it, a bird being able to fly is pretty incredible. How on earth do they stay up in the sky? Live television is mind-blowing too. How can the picture and sounds of one person sitting in a TV studio be transmitted into millions of homes every day? The internet is baffling. How do we get all that information at our fingertips every single day? The ability of a tree to move through the seasons and regenerate itself each year is fascinating. It's easy to forget that you are part of an extraordinary world – but if you forget, your children will remind you.

What you do every single day in caring for your children may seem quite ordinary. You are 'just' a mum who does the cooking and the cleaning and looks after your children. But you're not: you are so much more than this. You are the protector, the teacher and the entertainment crew. You are the most important person in your children's little worlds. You have made a choice to spend as much time as you possibly can with them so you can love them, support them and help them grow into the best people that they can become.

You are shaping the future generation of our society. And that is really quite extraordinary.

CHAPTER FOUR

How to Save Your Sanity

"Mothers are all slightly insane."

The Catcher in the Rye, JD Salinger

Staying at home and responding to the 24/7 demands of little people is exceptionally hard work. There can be times even the strongest person calls into question their own sanity when facing the day-to-day challenges of motherhood. I want to offer some advice and simple strategies to preserve your mind.

Build your mummy network

During your maternity leave, you probably made friends with other mums. Some of these will have decided to return to work and others will have decided to stay at home. These friendships will be incredibly important as your child grows up and you'll have a special bond with these women, from this significant period of your life.

Being at home with your kids on a permanent basis is very different to being on maternity leave. There is an air of excitement around maternity leave, particularly with your first child, as it is a time-limited period when you get used to the magical world of motherhood. It's a time when you take a break from the routine of going to work every day. To a certain extent, it can feel a little bit as if you are 'playing house'.

If you decide to not return to work after your maternity leave, life can feel very different, especially if all your friends do go back. That's when it's really important that you meet new people and get to know other mums who are in the same position as you.

"Being the only one of my NCT [antenatal class] group to not go back to work at all, and in the middle of winter, I did get lonely and lacked structure to my days at first. I knew this might happen and tried to mitigate it as soon as it happened by finding out all the local groups and classes my son and I could go to, but it still didn't fill the days. If we were at home most of the day, I found it hard to give my son my full attention and he would cause chaos!

Things got easier when a few friends started having second babies so were on maternity leave again, and as the weather got better and days got longer, so we could just go to the park to get out of the house. It's also easier (in some ways!) and less lonely now he can communicate so much more. Although I knew it would probably be the hardest part of being a stay-at-home-mum, that didn't make it any easier."

Stay-at-home mum of one

You may find that you have a lot in common with other stay-at-home mums and strike up friendships with people you wouldn't ordinarily have met. You may start wondering whether you need any more 'mum' friends. You don't want to spend all of your time talking to other women about their children, nappies, potty training, choosing schools etc. After all, you are a person in your own right, with your own passions and interests.

Conversations about your children are inevitable because that is the common bond that you all share. However, remember that other mums are real people too. They probably don't want to be solely focused on nappies and potty training any more than you do. You won't necessarily strike up a friendship with every single mum you meet, but eventually you will meet one or two kindred spirits.

Having local mums as friends can be a real sanity-saver when you're spending long days at home alone with your children. Being at home with your kids can be tough. From time to time everybody will find it difficult (even if they claim they don't). Having somebody close by that you can let off steam with can make life that little bit easier.

Having stay-at-home-mum friends locally can be a great source of practical support. Knowing that you have friends who can help you out, even with little run-around tasks like picking up a prescription when your child is unwell or dropping off an older child at nursery while you've got a newborn at home, is a huge relief. I live in a wonderfully supportive community with a strong network of 'mum friends' who help me out when I need it. Just knowing that there are people nearby is very reassuring, particularly as we have no family close to where we live.

If the thought of getting out there and meeting new people is daunting for you, here are a few tips on what you can do to make meeting other mums easier:

1. Be consistent. Try to go to the same activities e.g. toddler groups, classes etc. at the same time every week. To begin with, you will be a new face, but as you continue to attend you will become one of the regulars. Before you know it, you will know everybody and be showing the newcomers the ropes.

2. Even if it makes your toes curl at the very thought, strike up a conversation with the person sitting next to you whenever you go to a group event.

    a. A simple "Hello, I haven't been here before" is usually enough to get the conversation moving.

    b. Children make the perfect icebreakers. You could say something like "How old is your son/ daughter?" or "I love that jumper/ jacket/ those wellie boots. Where did you buy them?"

c. People love to be seen as experts and to give advice. You could say: "My son's hair really needs cut. I've been trying to find a good local hairdresser. Can you recommend someone?"

3. Go online. Love it or loathe it, social media has transformed the way we operate as a society. Most areas now have a local Facebook group for mums and this can be an amazing way to build links in your local community, particularly if you are quite shy about talking to people face to face.

If there isn't a group in your area, why not set one up? That is a sure-fire way of getting to know people so you can build your own network of mum friends and help other mums build theirs.

I set up a Facebook group for mums in my local area, which grew from nothing to 3,300 mums supporting and helping each other. I've since handed it over to somebody else to run, but I got to know loads of mums in my local community by starting it and have even developed some genuine, real-life friendships from it.

Spend time with the right people

As you build your mummy network, you will naturally gravitate towards mums that you have an affinity with and this will give you a great sense of support. Always make sure that you spend time with people who support you and who make you feel good about your decision to stay at home with your kids.

The wonderful thing about being at home with your children is that during the day you don't have to do anything that you don't want to do. If your day isn't going as you planned and you don't feel like going somewhere, then just don't do it.

There is nothing worse than being exhausted and grumpy because you have been up several times in the night with a child who will just **not** stay asleep, only to have to go out and listen to another mum regale you with stories of how wonderfully her child sleeps. You know the ones… They actually have to wake their children up in the morning. *Wake their children up!* This is after you have had to lie in bed desperate for the toilet, but you are too scared to move in case you disturb your little one and start your day at 4.32am!

Perhaps your children are good sleepers but I am sure that you have your own challenges to face. If you're having tough day then you don't need to hear about other parents' triumphs in that area! Be kind to yourself and minimise the time that you spend with 'perfect parents'.

Finely tune your bullsh*t filter

I highly recommend that all mums hone their bullsh*t filter. This isn't something exclusive to the stay-at-home mum, but because they spend more time around other parents, it is particularly important that they are able to spot when other parents are being less than truthful.

Parents lie. All parents lie. We can't help ourselves. We do it to a greater or lesser extent depending on our mood, our levels of sleep deprivation and who we are talking to. Some parents lie a lot. If little Jack really has slept through the night every single night without fail since he came home from hospital as a newborn, then he is an infant miracle. If Abigail, at the age of two-and-a-half, can recite the entire alphabet backwards in English and Spanish then we should be calling the Guinness Book of Records.

Some parents lie a little bit. You might tell Grandma that Harry loved that book she sent, when he took one look at it, saw that it had nothing to do with pirates (his obsession of the moment) and tossed it to one side. Perhaps you told your neighbour that baby Erin looks really pretty in that dress she bought, when you'd never ever put such a hideous outfit on your child.

> *"It used to really amuse me. There was one lady I would see every week at a toddler group. If you believed her, then her daughter was an angel who slept 14 hours a day and did absolutely everything that she was told. I had seen her husband wrestling with her on the floor of the swimming pool trying to get her to go into the water. I don't understand why the mum couldn't just tell the truth. No child is perfect. I know mine isn't."*
>
> Sally, stay-at-home mum of three

Sometimes parents lie for the greater good; sometimes

because they want the world to think that their child is the most special, talented and unique individual to have ever graced our planet. If you are spending a lot of time with other mums, you need to hone that bullsh*t filter so that you know when people are being economical with the truth. Otherwise you will be convinced that you have spawned the devil child and all the other little people around you are angels.

Find pockets of time just for yourself

I had an interesting conversation with a friend's husband recently. They were a month away from having their first baby and had decided to get a bit of practice in by agreeing to look after his 18-month-old niece for the day. He said he couldn't believe how completely and utterly exhausted he was at the end of the day. The niece had been perfectly well behaved, but she was 18 months old and demanded attention all day. He felt he constantly had to be 'on it' in case anything happened to her. By 5pm, he was completely drained.

Obviously, we had the jokey conversation, "Just you wait until your baby is born. Then you'll really know what tiredness is all about!" He was absolutely right, of course. When you're looking after young children, you are constantly 'on it'. This state of hypervigilance, always on the lookout for danger and trying to second-guess what mischief the little people are going to get up to, is completely and utterly exhausting.

While it may appear that you have only gone to the supermarket, your brain has had to process a hundred different thoughts and work through all the different options of what could potentially go wrong and how you could avoid it.

With this in mind, whenever you get the opportunity, make sure you take some time out just for yourself. If your children are still young enough to nap, resist the temptation to be productive during all of that nap time. Even if it's just ten minutes to sit quietly with a cup of tea, do it! You need to recharge your batteries so that you can keep on going for the rest of the day.

> *"I've started to read again. I used to always have a book on the go and would get through several books in a week when I was commuting. Now when Harry goes for a nap, I spend the first half-hour reading my book. I'll then do some housework. But if I read my book first, I know that even if he wakes up sooner than I expect I have still had a chance to 'escape' for a little while into my book. It's made such a difference to my day."*
>
> Vicky, stay-at-home mum of one

If your children are no longer napping then it can be harder to carve out some time for yourself, so try to get them engaged in a quiet activity for a while each day. Don't feel bad if you let them watch TV for a little while so you can have a few minutes to yourself. Yes, you did read that correctly. I said let them watch TV. I am not advocating leaving them in front of the electronic babysitter for hours on end, but you are human and every now and then you need a break. Twenty minutes of cartoons while you have a quick cuppa is not going stunt their intellectual development or lead to a lifetime of depravity. And remember, the housework and the emails that you need to return can wait because you need to take some time out just for you.

Get your house in order

As a stay-at-home mum, your number one priority is having a clean and tidy house, an empty laundry basket and a cooked meal on the table for your partner every evening.

Erm… yeah right!

We have already talked about the futility of trying to keep your house tidy while your children are young and ready to wreak havoc and destroy all of your good work in a moment. However, unless you want to feature in an episode of *Britain's Biggest Hoarders* or some other similar reality TV show, you do need to put in some effort to keep your house in order.

With that said, bear in mind that, just because you're the person who is around all day looking after the children, you aren't necessarily the one who has to do every single housekeeping task yourself. Remember, you did not give up your job to become a housekeeper; you gave up your job to look after your children.

You need to think sensibly about how you can divide up the household tasks between everyone who lives in the house. It may be a little unrealistic to ask your two-year-old to do the ironing, but think about who lives in your house and how can they contribute to keeping the place tidy and clean. Housework is dull, but it needs to be done.

If you need to draw up a rota to make it clear who does what or who is responsible for particular jobs, then do so. My husband would never begin to pretend that he knows when the kids are going to birthday parties, what's in the secret birthday present stash cupboard, or where the wrapping paper and Sellotape is kept. That is strictly my domain. On the other hand, when it comes to batteries, lightbulbs and smoke alarms, my husband magically takes care of all of these things.

Once you are clear which jobs are yours and which are someone else's, write them all down and chunk them into four or five batches so you can complete a batch of jobs each day of the working week – whatever that means for your household. Prioritise the tasks so that you always get the essential jobs done.

It might even be worth setting a time limit to get everything to a point that is 'good enough' for you, so you don't spend too much of your day on them. If you don't set clear boundaries for yourself, you could drive yourself crazy doing an endless round of jobs. Give yourself half an hour at the start of the day when your energy levels are high and get cracking so you get your jobs done early on. Little people always seem to be happier to entertain themselves in the morning, so let them rediscover their toys and create their own adventures while you get your chores underway. It will be much easier to do them earlier than later in the day when the kids are tired, cranky and need a lot more input from you.

Outsource

Some people find cleaning therapeutic, some people don't mind it and a lot of people (myself included) absolutely hate it. As a result, I have pretty low expectations of the cleanliness of my house and some would find my definition of 'good enough' questionable. I know that this will only be an option for the minority, but if you can afford it, there is absolutely nothing wrong with paying somebody else to clean your house. Don't be a martyr. If you hate housework and have the means to pay somebody else to do it, then for goodness sake get a cleaner!

If you can't afford it, but you're a housework hater, it might be worth thinking of a way that you can earn some extra money so that you can pay for a few hours of cleaning. I have spoken to many mums who think that people will call them lazy if they have somebody else cleaning their house. Who cares what other people think? If having a cleaner is a priority for you and you can afford it (or can come up with the money to pay for it from somewhere), don't be embarrassed about it. Your focus should be that the cleaning gets done by **_somebody_** and that your house is in a state that you are happy to live in.

Get your children involved

My children are like chalk and cheese in most respects and their attitudes to cleaning is no different. From an early age, my daughter trailed happily around the house doing jobs with me, chatting away and helping me with her own little cloth and spray. My son does not. On the odd occasion that he does want to get involved, he tends to empty the laundry all over the floor and then jump on it or he 'helps with the washing up' by climbing onto the work surface and filling the sink with water and flooding the kitchen. I'm not the best person to offer advice on how to get an uncooperative toddler to help keep the house tidy, but there are some strategies that I use to help get them involved tidying their toys:

- Use plastic storage boxes to organise small toys so that they don't end up at the bottom of the toy box.

- Have separate boxes for different types of toys. Help the children to recognise what these different boxes are and get them to tidy the toys away into the right boxes.

- Don't have all of their toys out and available to play with all of the time. If they have too much choice then they will end up playing with nothing at all and just get lost in the sea of brightly coloured plastic.

- Rotate the toys and books that you keep out for your children so that there is always something new and interesting for them to look at.

- Store the other toys and books out of the way so there is less for them to create a mess with. Also, when you bring them out again, they will seem new and interesting.

I always reward any efforts to tidy up with lots of praise, hugs and kisses. I'm hoping that rewarding even the most minimal effort will encourage them to help out more in the future. Really, really hoping... So cross your fingers for me!

Be kind to yourself

As women, we are often our own worst enemies. On the one hand, we expect too much of ourselves. On the other, we never take time to appreciate all that we do manage to achieve. It's a lose-lose situation.

"It is so rare that anyone tells you you're doing okay. I think it is so easy to be self-critical and when the children are in bed I evaluate my day thinking how I could have handled things better. You never praise yourself."

Stay-at-home mum of two

Modern life is busy for everybody. We have a multitude of

roles to fulfil and ridiculously high expectations of ourselves. Rather than celebrating all that we do manage to cram into our life, we berate ourselves for not doing or being enough. We torture ourselves by comparing our achievements with those of other people – like the mum who always has freshly baked cakes in the tin, the mum whose house is always spic-and-span and the mum who spends hours creating intricate crafts with her children. You don't need to be any of these women. You just need to be yourself.

It's also worth reminding yourself that you are only getting to see the version of events that other people want you to see. You've got no idea what is going on behind closed doors. From the outside, another family's life might look like a picture of domestic bliss but, in reality, life is probably not quite so perfect. All those mums you think are so effortlessly holding it all together probably have their own battles to fight. Your kids might not sleep through the night, but her kids might be fussy eaters. Nobody's family is perfect, despite what people might want you to believe.

"I have learned, that 'good enough' really is okay. You don't have to be perfect. Aiming for perfection will result in stress and unhappiness.

My kids don't want a perfect mum, turning out beautiful cupcakes, forever tidying and rushing and stressing out. They just want time, attention and love. I also now realise that I need to give myself a lot more credit for the small things that I achieve everyday (like getting everyone to school on time) and forgive myself for the things that sometimes go a bit wrong (like getting cross and shouting at the girls occasionally).

No-one is perfect and it is not a competition – it's okay if other mums are turning out beautiful cupcakes and I'm not."

Helen, mum of two
co-owner of Busy Lizzy, Reigate

Rather than comparing ourselves to others, wouldn't life be better if we just accepted ourselves and others for who we are?

"To be honest, I actually find it very boring playing games with children as I like to get things done and achieved. I have very little patience with teaching them stuff, so I am very happy when they have friends over and can entertain themselves and let me get on with housework/planning my own business etc."

Lucy Best, mum of two
and owner of Hampshire Orthotics

At the end of the day, we are all just doing the best that we can in our own perfectly imperfect way.

To help you appreciate how well you're doing, I would encourage you to make a note each evening of three things that you have achieved that day and three things that you are grateful for. This should take you no more than five minutes, but it's such a helpful reminder to celebrate your successes, no matter how small.

CHAPTER FIVE

Money, Money, Money…

There's no escaping it. Money is often the biggest worry for women who decide to stay at home with their children. Before having children, very few of us would ever have considered giving up work completely and relying on a single income to keep the household afloat. Add to that the fact that there will be at least one additional mouth to feed and the giving up of a steady income can look like lunacy.

Over the last few years, there has been a real shift in society's attitude to spending money. A combination of factors such as the global economic downturn, growing scepticism about the spend-spend-spend culture of the late nineties and early noughties, a desire to limit the impact on the environment, and an attempt to minimise consumption have led many families to do what they can to live within more meagre means.

> *"Children will not remember you for the material things you provided. But for the feeling that you cherished them."*
>
> Richard L Evans

Living on a reduced family income

If you have decided to stay at home with the kids and live on a smaller family income, you need to adjust your behaviour so that you only spend money on what you need rather than anything you want. The time will come when as a family you will have more disposable income and can spend money on life's little luxuries.

In the meantime, be grateful for what your family does have and appreciate that while times are tight, you have food on the table, clothes on your back and a roof over your head. That is much, much more than what many people in the world are able to enjoy. During this leaner period, there are three things that you can do to help your family finances:

- Spend less.

- Make the money that you do spend go further.

- Find ways to generate extra income.

Spend less

I appreciate that spending less is often easier said than done and temptation lies around every corner. But while the family coffers are running lower than usual, you need to be disciplined so you can make sure you live within your means.

"You will always live within your means, whatever the family income. We dropped £20,000 per year and were concerned about how we would cope. It

actually was easy and after 19 months we still don't miss the money. Our rewards are no longer holidays, meals out and luxuries, but in playing with Duplo, walks in the park, and feeding the ducks."

Stay-at-home mum of one

If you want to take control of your finances, the first step is to keep track of your spending. Record what you are spending your money on over the course of a month. Create a set of categories that work for your family and take note of the money you spend in each one. For example:

- Rent/mortgage.
- Utility bills.
- Grocery shopping.
- Clothes.
- Entertainment.
- Treats.

You will soon see where your money is going and also where you may be able to cut back and economise.

Sometimes, it is the little treats you buy that start to add up. These are the easiest expenses to cut because you hardly notice them on a day-to-day basis. For example, you may think the £1.50 you spend on coffee every time you go to the park is nothing to worry about, but if you go to the park four times a week, every week for a year, that will add up to over £300 a year – just on coffee. Once you realise how this small amount adds up, you can decide whether you want to spend £300 a year on coffee at the park or whether you would prefer to spend it on something else. When you have a handle on how you are spending your money, you will be in a better position to review the budget for your family.

I know that budgeting can be boring or that it might not be your strong point, but it is important. If you do need to reduce your outgoings, there are some simple steps you can take to get yourself started.

Use cash instead of cards

We live in an age of convenience and so we love our little plastic cards. However, according to Investopedia, on average, we spend 28% less when we use cash than credit cards, and 18% less with cash than debit cards. I know that cash is going out of fashion and I am very reliant on my debit card, but it makes perfect sense. When you use cash, you are more aware of the amount of money that you are spending.

Consider this scenario. You're on a rare day out away from the kids and you see a beautiful coat. It's just what you have been looking for but it costs £100 and is a bit more than you were planning to spend on a coat. You ask yourself, "Can I really justify spending £100 on a coat?" That little voice inside your head says, "Go on, treat yourself. Put it on the credit card and you can pay it off next month. You never buy anything new and how often do you get to go shopping anyway?" In this situation, you might be tempted to treat yourself to the coat, mightn't you?

Now imagine what would happen if you saw the £100 coat when you were out, but only had £80 of cash in your purse. It wouldn't matter how much you might love the coat, you wouldn't be able to afford it. If you only had £80 and the coat cost £100, you would have to leave it. You would not go over your budget and you would not be able to overspend.

Why not see for yourself how it feels to spend cash rather than using plastic? Take your cards out of your purse and just use cash for a few days. You will immediately witness your behaviour changing. When you spend cash, you are more likely to notice because you handle the money and see its value. When you only have a certain amount of cash available, you can't spend more than you've got.

Make one small change

If your budget feels tight, try making one small change in your spending habits. Simply look for one thing you buy every month that you can cut out. When you look through your bank statement, you will probably be able to identify at least one item you are paying for that you either don't need or that you're not getting the most from. Perhaps it's a gym membership that you only use twice a month. (Think how much you would save if you just paid for two trips to your local leisure centre.) Maybe you have a monthly contact lens plan, but you wear them so infrequently that you could buy some daily disposables in bulk every few months. No matter how small a saving you make, it will all add up.

Think before you buy

Contrary to popular belief, your little ones do not need to cost the earth. Although the baby and infant market has exploded in recent years, you don't need all of it. You can now buy everything from a Peepee Teepee (a little towelling device to stop baby boys peeing on you during nappy changes) to a set of fake hands to lay on your newborn so that they think they're being held (I fancied one of these when Boy Wonder was a baby but fortunately sanity prevailed!) Like I said, you don't need all of it!

There are so many items you *can* buy for your children and there are so many items you may *want* to buy for your children, but there is probably not much that you genuinely *need* to buy for your children. On top of that, we seem to be turning our children into consumers at a younger and younger age. In fact, advertisers are increasingly reliant on the pester power of children to badger their parents into buying everything they want.

However, small children have the incredibly annoying habit of neglecting their lovingly selected and often expensive toys in favour of normal household objects. It seems they can entertain themselves for hours with a box of curtain rings or an empty cardboard box.

> *"Despite having received countless new toys at Christmas time, my two-year-old has spent the morning playing with some clothes pegs and a bucket of water. I don't begrudge him the toys but I do sometimes wonder why we bother!"*
>
> Mel, stay-at-home mum of one

I'm not saying that you shouldn't buy your kids any toys at all, but at the same time, do bear in mind that they probably don't need as many as you think. Very young children won't know the difference between brand new, shiny, shop-bought toys and pre-loved toys that have been passed down from friends and family or have come from the charity shop. Children seem to accumulate a disproportionate amount of 'stuff' given how small they are. Friends with children will probably be delighted to pass on or sell you some of that 'stuff' to free up space in their home for the next influx of 'stuff' that is coming along.

You can also save a fortune by buying or accepting donations of second-hand clothes. This is easy when your children are younger and don't have a preference about what they wear. I am the first to admit that when Super Girl was born I had no intention of dressing her in hand-me-downs. Fast-forward five years and my attitude has completely changed. I now understand how quickly children grow out of clothes and how easy it is to buy something for them that only gets worn once or twice for one reason or another. Take advantage of the chance to buy second-hand clothes. You can pick up some serious bargains and the clothes often look as good as new.

Top tips for finding bargain kids' toys and clothes:

- eBay – the fall-back for bargain-hunting parents.

- Gumtree – particularly good when you want to find a larger item that you can pick up locally.

- Local Facebook groups – the number of mums' networks and selling groups on Facebook has exploded in the last few years. This is an excellent way to help support mums in your local area and find some bargains at the same time.

- NCT sales – particularly good for baby clothes and equipment.

- Local baby and toddler sales – Cheeki Monkeys, Little Pickles Markets, Mum 2 Mum Markets and Bumps to Babies Markets.

- Your mummy network – don't be afraid to ask mums with older children if they are looking to sell unwanted clothes or toys. They are unlikely to be offended and are often delighted at the opportunity to clear some space in their house and make some money with minimal effort.

"I couldn't believe it. Shortly after we moved into our house, my neighbour appeared at our door with two

bin liners full of toys. They had older children and were doing a big clear-out and thought we could get some use out of their old toys. It was amazing. All of it was in fantastic condition and it saved us a fortune!"

Vicky, stay-at-home mum of two

Ask for what you want

Friends and family can be incredibly generous when it comes to buying for children. If you know people are planning to give a gift anyway (and you know you won't offend them), don't be embarrassed about giving suggestions about what your children want or need. It would be such a shame for them to waste money on a gift that your children wouldn't particularly appreciate when there are plenty of ideas for what they would benefit from or enjoy.

Make your money go further

I have absolutely no doubt that if you are living on a reduced income then you will be keeping an eye on the pennies and making sure that you get the most from your money. Here are some tips I've picked up over the past few years:

Spend to save

If you have the space – and the opportunity – then it is

seriously worth considering buying some items in bulk. Don't be seduced by all of the supermarket buy-one-get-one-free offers. You're not saving money if you buy products that you don't use. However, stocking up on household products such as toilet roll, washing up liquid and baby essentials like nappies and wipes while they are on special offer makes a lot of financial sense. Although making large purchases might eat into your budget for a particular week, it will pay off in the long run.

Plan, plan, plan

Even if you are not one of the world's natural planners, try to take some time to work out what your meals are going to be for the week. Taking the time to decide what you are going to eat means you can create a shopping list with exactly what you need on it. This will save you money when you get to the supermarket because you can make sure that you only buy what you're going to use.

For example, if a recipe needs half a bunch of fresh coriander, think about what you can do with the rest of the bunch. Could you double up the quantity of the recipe and freeze half for another day? Batch cooking is a great way of making sure you have home-made nutritious food ready on those days when you don't have time to cook. If you have the space, it might be worth investing in a second freezer. You can very often find old freezers on Gumtree or eBay for very reasonable prices, or if you're very lucky, get one free on Freecycle.

Minimise waste

Take a good look through your fridge and cupboards. How much food do you throw away? Are there things that you keep on buying but never use? Don't just keep putting things on your shopping list because you're used to buying them. If you're spending money on something, make sure that you're using it.

Make the most of home delivery

I know a lot of people are not keen on online shopping because of the cost of having their groceries delivered. However, online shopping can be a great way to economise on your weekly shop.

If you shop online, you can create an account and save your favourite items. This means you'll be more focused on your favourites list each week rather than getting distracted by special offers. It also means you can monitor your shopping basket, so if you find you're spending too much, you can delete some items before you go through the checkout process.

You can get cheaper delivery by choosing a less popular slot – usually a time when most other people are at work. You can offset the delivery fee by saving on the cost of petrol and parking, and by focusing on your favourites. The other benefit is that you can avoid the stress of trying to do a big shop while accompanied by young children.

Bag a bargain

There is now a wide range of websites that can keep you updated on the latest offers available. It's worth staying up-to-date with special offers via websites such as Money Saving Expert and Bargain Buys for Busy Mums, as well as keeping abreast of offers from major retailers and voucher code sites so you can save as much money as possible.

Generate some extra income

There are lots of ways that you can generate extra income from home. I'm not talking about starting a business. We'll explore that in more detail in Chapter 10, Start Your Own Business. However, if you're enterprising, there are plenty of ideas for making that little extra amount of money to make things more comfortable.

Sell your stuff

Try to view everything that you have as an asset. When times are tight, think about how you can release money from what you own.

Kids grow quickly, which means they grow out of clothes, games and toys at warp speed. There are also lots of parents out there who need to buy these items for their children, but either don't want to buy them new or are unable to afford them new. This means there is a ready market for second-hand children's stuff. You can sell items for a low commission on eBay or free on Gumtree as well as on local Facebook groups.

If you have a big garden and grow your own fruit and vegetables or you have chickens who lay more eggs than you can use, you could sell your surplus produce on a stall outside your house. You could also sell plant cuttings, bulbs and herbs. If you don't want to sit at your stall all day, just leave an honesty box on the table so people can pay you when you're not around.

There are now specialist websites that buy old mobile phones, CDs and computer games. This is another great way to get rid of stuff you no longer want, but that can be useful to others. When you sell your unwanted items, it's win-win, because you give others the opportunity to get what they need at a lower price than usual and you make some money at the same time.

Make the most of your space

If you have a spare room, you could rent out a room to a boarder or an exchange student. Language schools often need to find short-term accommodation for students. This could be a good solution if you don't want somebody living with you permanently, but are happy to take a student or two for a few weeks at a time. It's also a great way to expose your children to new languages and cultures.

If you are close to a railway station, airport or popular amenity, you could rent out your driveway or garage for someone to park in.

Just Park, Park Let and Your Parking Space are all great resources that can help you find people interested in renting out your parking space.

Having your own money

Having your own money can be a huge issue for some stay-at-home mums. It's important that you discuss this with your partner so you can manage your own personal financial situation and find a solution that works for both of you.

When I decided I wasn't going to return to paid employment after I finished my maternity leave, I was concerned about how I was going to feel about not having my own income. After Super Girl was born, though, I started to realise how hard I was going to have to work if I stayed at home and didn't return to work. At that point, I suddenly became very comfortable with the idea that my husband's salary was our money. We were both contributing to making our family work so we both earned it.

How you organise your money with your partner depends on your attitudes and the agreement you make together. It is possible that you will feel completely at ease using money from your joint account whenever you want to buy something. However, if you feel guilty about dipping in to your joint funds, you might prefer to allocate a set amount of money to yourself each month so you know you can spend it as you wish, guilt-free.

If you worry that you haven't earned this money, bear in mind that although your partner might be the one who is going out to earn the cash to support your family, you are at home working to take care of your children and providing for your family in other ways. You have both earned it, just differently.

"The thing I found the hardest about being at home was not having any money to call my own. To begin with, I wouldn't spend any money on myself at all. Eventually, my husband asked why I wasn't getting haircuts and getting my nails done the way I used to.

We then had a really good chat about how I felt and agreed that I should set aside a sum of money every month that was just for me. Sometimes I spend all of it, other times I save it. It's just nice to know there is a little pot of money to dip into if I need it."

Verity, stay-at-home mum of one

You work very hard in an extremely demanding, time-consuming and often stressful job. You deserve a treat once in a while. You might not be able to afford everything you used to have when you were in your job, but a new haircut or outfit from time to time will boost your morale and will be a very, very well-deserved treat.

CHAPTER SIX

Your Relationships

"When you become a parent, you look at your parents differently. You look at being a child differently. It's an awakening, a revelation that you have."

Philip Seymour Hoffman

The way that you interact with the world and the people around you will inevitably change when you have a child. Your priorities and mindset have shifted. So too have your relationships with your partner, family and friends.

Your partner

Do you remember that person who you were once so in love with that you decided to embark on this parenthood malarkey with them? When children come along, it's easy for all of us to lose sight of our other half. We get so wrapped up in family life that we often forget about our partner. I'm not talking about the person that is now known as Daddy, but the person that you fell in love with.

When was the last occasion you spent some proper time with your partner, just the two of you?

Inevitably, your relationship with your partner changes when you have children. Where you once spent hours enjoying each other's company and spending interesting time together, you now spend hours caring for your children. Your lives revolve around the little people, when they have to be fed, watered, changed, dropped off or picked up. You spend time talking about whether there is enough money coming in to meet your family's needs. All of a sudden, you have become proper 'grown-ups' with real responsibilities.

Having children is a huge shift for both of you and takes a lot of getting used to. You are no longer each other's number one priority. There is another little person (or people) around that you both love to the ends of the earth and would do anything to protect. As a result, it's all too easy to forget why you got together in the first place. When you are weary from the day-to-day monotony of family life, you often don't have time for each other.

To balance out the situation, make sure you carve out some time to spend together as a couple. When your children are very young, this can be hard, especially if you don't live near family or have babysitters on tap. You could consider setting up a babysitting circle with friends and taking turns to look after each other's children so that you can have a well-deserved night off without the additional cost of childcare.

If getting a babysitter isn't an option then even something as simple as committing to having a meal together once the kids have gone to bed can make a difference: a real meal, sitting at a table, maybe even with some candles and music so you can have a proper conversation and spend some quality time together. Sitting slumped in front of the TV when you're too tired to move or talk doesn't count!

Make the effort for each other. Keep your relationship alive and take some time out to remember why you embarked on this amazing adventure called parenthood together. It will stand you in good stead as your children grow and you take on each new challenge as they develop.

Being the partner of a stay-at-home mum

I am sure that your decision to stay at home with the kids involved long and lengthy conversations with your partner, weighing up the pros and cons and working out what was going to be right for your family. I genuinely hope that your partner was supportive of your decision to stay at home with your children. If your partner is fully supportive of your decision to stay at home, this will make life much easier.

Deciding to stay at home with the kids, putting your career on hold and giving up your 'old life' is a massive step for you. That being the case, it's easy to forget it's also a massive step for your partner too. Your partner may become the sole breadwinner of the household and bear all responsibility for the rent/mortgage, household bills and keeping the family afloat financially. That is a lot of pressure for one person.

As the stay-at-home parent, we often spend so much time worrying about the transition we are going through that we forget what a big adjustment it is for our partner as well. It's easy to forget when we are tired and frustrated after a long day of childcare that they have also had trying situations and people to deal with. They have often had to negotiate tedious journeys to and from work and now have much less time to pursue their own interests and hobbies.

"I really do feel guilty. My husband is out at work all day, tired, stressed, while I'm at home with our child where he would very much like to be."

Harriet, stay-at-home mum of one

You might watch your partner with envy as he leaves the house every morning. He gets to go to work, do 'important things', make a difference and (dare I say it) actually achieve something tangible with his day. His contribution is valued by others. People thank him when he has done a good job. He earns a salary. He gets to sit down and eat lunch in peace. He gets to interact socially with other adults all day long and sometimes might even get to catch up with friends for a drink on the way home.

When you're up to your eyeballs in nappies, rejected meals and laundry, it can feel like you and your partner live in two completely different worlds, especially if you have barely had an adult conversation all day. Talk to your partner. Find out how he feels about potentially being the sole earner. You are both working hard every single day, playing your part and making your contribution to the family. Take time to acknowledge and appreciate the work that you both do for the people you care about most.

Your parents

When you become a parent yourself, you will probably find that you start to re-evaluate your attitude to your close family, especially your own parents. It's difficult to understand at first, but the way you feel about your children is exactly how your parents feel about you. Once upon a time, you were a helpless baby and your parents held you just as you hold your own little one. They were just as completely overawed that they had managed to create something so wonderful and amazing as you feel by your own children.

In her beautifully written book *Late Fragments*, Kate Gross describes her relationship with her parents and her realisation of the strength of feeling that her parents had for her:

> *"I hadn't seen the kids since I had been admitted to A&E the night before. I rushed to give the sweaty, slightly odorous boys a hug. Obviously, they resisted my cuddles and I was left to ruffle their tousled heads while they told me purposefully about snakes and a*

> *fight with Fletcher. Mum hugged my arm while I was mid hair-ruffle. For an instant, I viewed my life from outside, as if it were a home movie. Mum looked at me the way I looked at them."*

Your children and new status as a mum may bring you closer to your parents than ever before. This might be because you feel a common bond with them now that you understand what it feels like to be a parent, or for more practical reasons, simply because you're spending much more time with them than before.

Your decision to stay at home and look after your children may well have been influenced by the relationship that you have with your parents. Perhaps your mum stayed at home with you and you're determined to give your own children the same start in life. But the opposite may also apply. If your own mother was a high-flying career woman and you constantly craved her presence and company, it may make your own resolve to stay at home even stronger.

Your parents may worry about your decision to stay at home. They may be concerned that you're 'wasting your education' or 'giving up' your hard-won place on the career ladder. You might feel frustrated by your parents' seeming lack of support about your decision. But if you stop and think about it, you will realise that you are *their* precious baby. It makes perfect sense that they are protective and concerned for you – just as you are for your little one. They want what is best for you and will never stop worrying about you. So reassure them that this decision wasn't made on a whim, that you have thought through the implications and know that you're making the right choice for your family.

Your friends

During your journey through the world of mumdom, you will more likely than not pick up new friends and acquaintances along the way. Each phase of the journey will bring new people into your life, but it's important not to forget your old friends – you know, the ones who knew you BC. These are the people who'll remember a more carefree and reckless version of you; the companions who have seen you through good times and bad.

Many of your friends will embark on their own journey of parenthood. Some may have done it already. This can bring a new dimension to your relationship. You can support each other along the way as you progress through this exciting and daunting journey together. They might be further along the parenting journey than you and can provide valuable insights – they can answer some of the questions you don't dare ask the experts or some of those newer friends. Equally, you may be further along the journey than some of your old friends, becoming a guiding light for them as they grapple with the same parenting dilemmas that you've already dealt with.

The friends who don't have children may find it difficult to adjust to the shift in your priorities after your children come along. They may struggle to understand the all-consuming nature of parenthood and find it hard to believe that you genuinely no longer have the time available for them that you once had.

Again, Kate Gross sums up beautifully the changing nature of friendships once children come along. She refers to her close friends as her 'Terracotta Army':

> *"Friendships survive on scraps of time and emails, squeezed between the rest of life and very often conducted thousands of miles apart. We live off well-trodden stories, the space in our lives for making new memories mostly taken up by family and work, where the real drama happens. The odd dinner, more often a cup of tea balanced precariously over a baby's head while we converse, but never enough time for the real stuff, or the new adventures together."*

When your children are young, it can be difficult to fit in those new adventures with old friends. Your decision to not return to your old job may make it even more challenging for those adventures to happen, but true friendships that are built on strong foundations will stand the test of time. With your closest friends, you will have an unbreakable bond. And while you might not be able to spend as much time together as you once did, when you have more time, you will quickly be able to pick up where you left off.

Your decision to stay at home with your children may bemuse some of your friends, while others may applaud you. True friends will support you whether they think that you are doing the right thing or not.

CHAPTER SEVEN

Your Confidence

"Believe in yourself. Have faith in your abilities.
Without a humble but reasonable confidence in
your powers, you cannot be successful or happy."

Norman Vincent Peale

How you feel about your decision to stay at home with
your children will very much influence how other people
approach it; they will take their cue from you, so make
sure you are comfortable with what you're doing. How do
you react when somebody that you've never met before
asks, "So, what do you do for a living?" Often, stay-at-
home mums dread this question.

We live in a funny old world. Modern society places so
much value on the status bestowed upon us by our job
that it's not uncommon to feel disconnected when we
no longer have one. If you're not going out to work and
earning a salary and you can't define yourself by your
job title, what value do you bring to the world? We are
identified by our career and other people's respect for
that career. Without it, who are we? Many stay-at-home
mums start to wonder about this same question:

without that job role, who am I?

In today's society, money and the ability to earn money seems to be the most immediate way to gain respect and status. But where does this leave stay-at-home mums who work long hours for the benefit of their family, yet earn nothing? Many women end up answering the 'what do you do?' question by saying they're 'just' a mum. But that word 'just' belittles the hard work, dedication and vast array of skills needed to be a stay-at-home mum.

> *"I find it hard to explain to others why I haven't gone back to work. I feel the need to justify my decision to be a stay-at-home mum. I find myself explaining about how my old commute wasn't feasible, saying how I'm starting my own business, which I feel the need to use as an excuse about what I'm spending my time on... As though raising children isn't good enough to be a full-time job!"*
>
> Harriet, stay-at-home mum of one

> *"I found it hard to lose my 'status' in the world. I felt this very keenly and although I wouldn't have done anything differently, I feel like a secret person, the forgotten one that used to be useful and have valued opinions, but now just empties the dishwasher!"*
>
> Emma, stay-at-home mum of two

Lead by example

To maintain healthy relations and positive reactions, you must lead by example. If you want other people to value you and your role, seeing it in a good light, you need to feel right about your decision to stay at home. Learn how to portray your role positively. After all, if you can't be upbeat about staying at home with your kids, how can you expect other people to feel positive about it? If **you** think that you're 'just' a mum, other people will think you're 'just' a mum too.

Most people, particularly those who do not have children, have absolutely no idea about the amount of work involved in staying at home to look after the kids. Many people automatically assume that stay-at-home mums have a limited education and weren't doing particularly important jobs in their previous life. For many woman, the situation is the exact opposite of this. Many stay-at-home mums are highly educated and successful career women who are taking a break from their career or have decided to not return because they think it's the right path for their family. Take pride in what you do. Believe that you are more than 'just a mum' and people will treat you that way.

To turn theory into reality, spend some time thinking about your response to the question: what do you do? Practise your response. Look in the mirror and say it out loud. This may sound a bit silly, but the more confidently you respond to this question, the more assertive you will be when you are asked the question.

Trust your instincts

This topic isn't solely the territory of women who stay at home with their children but it's an important one. I spent my twenties surrounded by confident, bright, articulate women who, when presented with a challenge, would assess it from all angles and tackle it head on.

I am now spending my thirties surrounded by the same women, but they are less confident. Much less confident. They have entered the world of parenthood and everything is new and scary. There's something massive at stake. The life and well-being of the most precious person in their world. They take hours to trawl the internet for magic cures for their baby's ills and spend inordinate amounts of money on the latest gadget that will be 'just the thing' to cure little Michael's colic.

I know exactly how they feel. For a short period of time, I was one of them. Having responsibility for another person's life is massive, especially when that other person is a vulnerable newborn who completely relies on you for everything.

As your baby grows, so too does your confidence, but as your child moves from one stage of development to another, you are back to being a newbie again. Once you've mastered the newborn phase, you're then thrown into teething, then crawling (and the job of baby-proofing your home) and then toddlerhood. It feels like you never have time to fully master one phase before you're moving on to the next.

Shortly after Super Girl was born, a friend (who was a bit further on the parenting journey) said to me, "You are the best mum in the world for Super Girl – nobody knows her the way that you do and nobody else in the world can make her feel as safe as you do." And she was absolutely right.

I could consult Dr Google to my heart's content (I think every modern-day new mum is guilty of obsessing over Dr Google), but on the few occasions when there was something seriously wrong with her, I knew I didn't need to look on the internet. I knew something wasn't right and we needed help. And we always got the help we needed, but no matter which doctor we consulted or which family member came to visit, it was always me that she wanted.

We come from a generation that considers it normal to consult parenting books about every single step of our child's development. There is so much conflicting advice out there that we could easily tie ourselves up in knots for days and never move forward. But I believe that deep down we know all of the answers ourselves. When it comes to our children, we are the experts. We know them better than anyone else in the world. We might need some specialist advice from a doctor on a medical condition or a teacher on a behavioural issue, but at the most basic level we know what's right for our little ones.

"It is so confusing! You ask a question and you get so many different responses. The health visitor says one thing, my mum says another. I've bought a few baby

sleep books. Some say that I should leave her to cry.
Others tell me that will damage her emotionally.
What on earth should I do?"

Claire, stay-at-home mum of one

Could it be we've lost confidence in ourselves and our ability to know what our child needs? A new, vulnerable parent is a marketer's dream, ripe for the picking. Eager to purchase that tried-and-tested solution that will make their child sleep through the night or help them meet all of their developmental milestones on time.

In the first few weeks of Super Girl's life, I must have spent hundreds of pounds on stuff I thought would help her to sleep better and longer. I bought a blanket made out of bamboo because another mother in my antenatal group had one and her daughter loved it. (Apparently, they couldn't leave home without it.) Her daughter was three weeks old and probably had no idea if she was sleeping on bamboo or cotton wool! It was soft and snuggly and she was a good sleeper anyway. I bought special bolsters to keep Super Girl in one position in her Moses basket (because obviously the reason she kept waking up was because she was banging on the sides of the Moses basket) and a sheepskin liner for the car seat (another soft and snuggly place for her to rest her head).

Do you know where she slept best? In my arms – of course! But everything I read and obsessively googled told me how harmful this was for my baby. Apparently, I needed to teach her how to sleep on her own or I was going to set her up for a childhood of bad sleeping habits. Well, maybe I was.

When she was around three months old, I threw out the parenting books. I stopped googling (except when illness was involved) and I cuddled her to sleep. Sometimes I put her down when she was asleep and sometimes I would sit and cuddle her while she slept. Sometimes I took the chance to nap when she napped or I just caught up on emails.

In short, I just trusted my instincts. I trusted that I was doing right by both of us. And while at times I felt trapped by this baby who needed me so much, I also look back on those times with fond memories. I realised that there are no tried-and-trusted solutions that will get our children to behave in a certain way and no developmental milestones are set in stone. We just need confidence in ourselves, belief that we're doing what's right for our little people and the sense to call in the real experts when we need more help.

Inject confidence boosts into your life

The longer you stay at home with your children the more likely it is that your confidence will get eroded – this can become a real issue as time goes on and will manifest itself in all sorts of ways.

The longer you're away from the workplace, the more you start to question your ability to return to it and get a job again. The longer you go without earning your own income, the more likely you are to question how you will ever be able to achieve your old salary again. That means you risk the temptation to accept any low-paid, low-status work that comes your way because you have no idea who else is going to employ you.

You may never have lost your baby weight after having your children, your confidence in your appearance has dipped. After years of being at home and not getting dressed for work on a daily basis, you may question your ability to spruce up and wear nice clothes again. And if you tend to spend a lot of your time with your 'mummy network', you may start to doubt your ability to have conversations with people in a business setting about topics other than your children.

Confidence is like a muscle: the more you use it, the stronger it becomes. While you're at home with your kids, you need to find ways to build and maintain your confidence so you don't lose it. One way to do this is to put yourself in positions that stretch and challenge you on a regular basis. We all have areas where we struggle. Get to know yours so you can work on them and enjoy feeling good about yourself. Be honest with yourself and think about the things you find difficult and perhaps situations that you shy away from. Identify ways that you can put yourself 'out there', experiences where you can start to rebuild your confidence. Keep working on these areas to rebuild your confidence. Keep working on them and soon you will start to enjoy feeling good about yourself again.

Get involved

A powerful way to build your confidence is to grab the bull by the horns and get involved in the world around you. Being at home with young children can be a lonely business, but there are opportunities everywhere for you to contribute your skills, experience and time either in your local community or in a wider context.

You could help out at a toddler group, become involved in the running of your pre-school, volunteer for a charity, spend time reading at a local school, drop off meals and do grocery shopping for local elderly neighbours. If contributing to local causes doesn't appeal to you, perhaps you could join a group that allows you to pursue an interest or a hobby. There are countless opportunities for you to get out there and contribute.

> *"Stay at home with your kids but don't be an island. Get involved. There is a whole new world of mumdom out there. Work it!"*
>
> Emma, stay-at-home mum of two

By getting yourself 'out there' and being involved in something that extends past the four walls of your house and the 24/7 demands of your children, you will feel part of something bigger. You will have the opportunity to work with other people and potentially be part of a team, all of which are great for building your confidence and self-esteem.

Be kind

Keep an eye out for the mums around you. Perhaps you can help another mum in your toddler group when she's struggling because her child never naps. You might be able to support the mum at the school gates whose child cries every single day that he goes into the classroom, or maybe you can befriend the young mum who always seems to be on her own at the playground. Keep an eye out for these women. They are everywhere and you will inevitably come across them in your daily life.

When you see them, share a kind word, show that you understand how hard they are working, and help them realise that what they're doing is appreciated. It doesn't take much, perhaps a few seconds of your time, but it could completely change somebody's day and perhaps even their whole attitude towards their situation.

CHAPTER EIGHT

Look After Yourself

"Whether you are a stay-at-home mum, or on the red carpet, or in Afghanistan, the better you feel, the better you do your job."

Bobbi Brown

It's important to remember that if you are not a happy mum you are unlikely to be able to create a happy family. You need to follow the life jacket principle. If an aeroplane is about to crash, you're told to always put on your own life jacket before helping anybody else with theirs. It's the same with being a mum: you need to put your own well-being at the top of your priority list so that you're in the best possible position to help your family.

When your children are young, you may feel there is no time to look after yourself, but this is far from true. In fact, you need to make looking after yourself a priority and find time to do it, even if it's just for ten minutes a day.

There is an interesting story that is often relayed in

business books about making time for the things that are important in our life. I think it successfully illustrates how it's possible for us to make time to look after ourselves even when it seems we don't have any.

One day, a visiting professor was speaking to a group of business students and, to drive home a point, he used the following illustration.

As this man stood in front of the group of high-powered over-achievers he said, "Okay, time for a quiz". Then he pulled out a one-gallon, wide-mouthed Mason jar and set it on a table in front of him. Then he produced about a dozen fist-sized rocks and carefully placed them, one at a time, into the jar.

When the jar was filled to the top and no more rocks would fit inside, he asked, "Is this jar full?" Everyone in the class said, "Yes." Then he said, "Really?" He reached under the table and pulled out a bucket of gravel. Then he dumped some gravel in and shook the jar causing pieces of gravel to work themselves down into the spaces between the big rocks.

Then he smiled and asked the group once more, "Is the jar full?" By this time, the class was onto him. "Probably not," one of them answered. "Good!" he replied. And he reached under the table and brought out a bucket of sand. He started dumping the sand in and it went into all the spaces left between the rocks and the gravel. Once more he asked the question, "Is this jar full?"

"No!" the class shouted. Once again he said, "Good!" Then he grabbed a pitcher of water and began to pour it in until the jar was filled to the brim.

Then he looked up at the class and asked, "What is the point of this illustration?"

One eager beaver raised his hand and said, "The point is, no matter how full your schedule is, if you try really hard, you can always fit some more things into it!"

"No," the speaker replied, "That's not the point. The truth this illustration teaches us is: if you don't put the big rocks in first, you'll never get them in at all."

Looking after ourselves needs to be one of these big rocks. We need to put that big rock in our jar and carve out a slot of time each week that is for us and us alone. Use it any which way you want, but it is **your time**. Protect it fiercely. You're not being selfish. This is about self-preservation.

Looking after babies and toddlers doesn't last forever. Before long your little ones will be off to nursery then school and be more independent. When this happens, you will have more time for yourself and you will be able to do more of what you want to do. You just need to keep your sanity through the toddler stage, safe in the knowledge that there will be more time for you as your children get older.

Your physical health

If you are unwell, it will be harder for you to care for your children. If you're feeling unhappy about something, your children will pick up on it. Your health and well-being impacts the entire household. You need to look after both.

Although it might be the last thing you feel like doing after a busy day running around looking after your children, try to build some exercise into your weekly routine. There are lots of buggy-fit classes that you can go to. If you have a very young child that is happy to sit in a pram, this is a great way to get some exercise and meet other mums at the same time.

You may be somebody who hates structured 'exercise', but there are still plenty of ways that you can remain active. Walking is a fabulous way of getting your body moving and building activity and fresh air into your day. When your children are still young enough to be in a pushchair, this is the perfect way to build 'exercise' into your day.

Keeping active and fit is highly important for your health and energy levels. It's also a great way to maintain your self-esteem. Here are some ideas that might help motivate you into action:

- Write a list of reasons to be more active – identify a goal, perhaps an event or a holiday that you want to get in shape for.

- Find an exercise regime that works for you. Be

realistic about it. If your partner doesn't get home until late in the evening, are you really going to get motivated enough to go to an exercise class when he gets home? Would you be better off investing in some short exercise DVDs or finding some workout videos on YouTube that you can fit in to short pockets of time?

- Get a friend to join in so you have somebody to exercise with (it'll be more fun and having someone else around will stop you making excuses).

- Plan rewards for when you achieve a particular goal or milestone. You might treat yourself to a massage when you swim X lengths in Y time or a trip to the cinema after completing a 5km fun run.

- Make it easy for yourself to exercise – lay out your exercise clothes the night before, pack your gym bag and keep it in the car, or invest in a waterproof jacket so that you can continue to walk everywhere even when it rains. Do whatever it takes to avoid procrastination.

Make the effort to eat well, too. If you find yourself snatching cold, uneaten fish fingers from your child's plate because you forgot to have lunch, why not make the most of your time at home to cook healthy, nutritious meals? That way, everybody wins. We all know that eating the right food fuels our body and a healthy diet will give you the energy you need to look after your family.

Your mental health

I approach this topic with trepidation as I am in no way qualified to comment on or provide advice about mental health. If you feel that you are seriously struggling with being at home with your kids then please, please, please talk to somebody. Your GP is a good place to start and can refer you elsewhere if necessary.

Sadly, post-natal depression appears to be on the rise. A recent study by Prima Baby used the system employed by doctors (the Edinburgh Scale) to check for PND symptoms. If a woman experiences five or more symptoms either all the time or for more than two weeks together, she is given a diagnosis of PND. Of 4,135 women who were tested, one in five fell into this category and 65% had experienced the symptoms of PND 'sometimes'. The Department of Health has estimated that one in ten women suffered from PND at some point.

Even if you do not fall into the category of PND, you can still feel overwhelmed by the challenges of day-to-day life with young children. If you feel stressed or your mood is low, here are some strategies to help you feel better:

- Try to look at a situation with a fresh perspective. For example, rather than, "I'm trapped at home all day", try thinking "I have no fixed commitments and am completely free to structure my day any way I want".

- Ask yourself: in 10 years' time, will this issue still matter to me?

- Draw on your support network. Having a support network of people who understand the situation you're in is important when you're at home all day with young children. Friends who work will only be able to understand how you feel up to a point.

- Enough exercise, while possibly the last thing you feel like doing, will make a big difference to your state of mind. It changes the chemical balance of your brain and raises your endorphin level so you feel better.

- Treat yourself! You may be living on a tight budget, but give yourself a small reward, even if it's just a coffee with a friend or some nice bath oil.

- Sleep... It's amazing how eight hours of uninterrupted sleep can shift your perspective.

Again, I cannot stress this enough: if you feel you are struggling, please talk to somebody and get the help you need. If you had a lump on your breast, you wouldn't hesitate to see a doctor. The same should be true with your mental health.

Take some time to be you

As soon as you manage to carve out some time for yourself, you probably feel so exhausted that all you want to do is sit on the couch, watch mindless TV and eat chocolate. It is tempting to give in to tiredness and not do anything with your time away from the children. But if you do make the effort to get out and do something different, you will feel much better about yourself.

Getting out of the house is crucial. It's lovely to have a bath or just enjoy some peace and quiet to read a good book, but there's something liberating about leaving the house and going out without the kids in tow. When you're on your own, you don't need to worry about whether you'll be able to fit a buggy through the doors, or plan ahead by taking a stack of snacks in your handbag, or worry that your toddler is going to cause havoc in a crowded area. You can go out, relax, enjoy yourself and truly be you.

Do you remember that time before the children came along? It may seem like a dim and distant memory now, but you used to be an independent person (with what now seems like endless free time). What did you used to do with all of that spare time? What did you enjoy doing?

It can be all-too-easy to lose yourself in the world of mumdom, constantly at the beck and call of other people. Yet, you *are* an individual in your own right and you need to be that person sometimes. When you get time away from your children, try to spend some of it with people who don't know you in your role as a mum. Maybe you could meet old friends that you knew before you had children or with people you got to know through sharing a common interest. Spending time with others as you The Individual, not you The Mum, allows you to let your own personality shine through, at least for a while.

> *"I sometimes miss the social side of working outside the home, especially around Christmas. My work functions now include around 20 children, jugs of squash and pass the parcel."*
>
> Kirstie, stay-at-home mum of two

If you feel that you're not getting the intellectual stimulation that you need during the day, you could take an evening class or join a book group. Whatever you do, try to find an activity that you find intellectually stimulating or where you can use your mind. You will more than likely go back home refreshed, recharged and looking forward to seeing your children again.

Taking the time to be you is important, but you are the only person who can make it happen. Identify a specific time every week that is your time. Ensure your partner/family knows how important it is that you have this time just for yourself. You are not being selfish or abandoning your family; you are doing what you need to do to maintain your sense of identity. Enjoy it!

CHAPTER NINE

Future-Proof Yourself

"But kids don't stay with you if you do it right. It's the one job where, the better you are, the more surely you won't be needed in the long run."

Barbara Kingsolver

"What a waste".

That's often a line that stay-at-home mums hear when they tell people about their decision to look after their kids full-time. What about the hard work that you've put in to your education? What about all the years you spent building your career? How can you turn your back on it all?

There's a huge misconception that stay-at-home mums are just throwing away their careers, and wasting a well-earned education and hard-won position on the corporate ladder. Just because you decide to spend a period of time out of the workplace looking after your children doesn't mean that your career is over. Far from it. Your working life doesn't need to end when you become a stay-at-home mum. You are still the same person. Spending time at home will not erase the education and experience that you have gained or eradicate the person that you are; you're simply taking time out to care for your family for a while.

Consider this: on average, a person can expect to be economically active for approximately 50 years of their life. So even if you decide to stay at home with your kids for five years that's still only 10% of your working life. You still have the other 90% to spend engaged in the rat race, if that's what you choose.

Stay connected with the world of work

If you would like to return to your old profession – or want to keep that door open – then it's well worth putting in a bit of work to make sure you're in the best position possible when the time comes to return to work. When you're at home, it can be tempting to think that your working life was a different lifetime. Sometimes you will romanticise it or miss the freedom and independence you recall it gave you. At other times, it will seem like an alien lifestyle that you can't possibly imagine returning to. Someday, however, you might want to do just that.

If you do, you want to make sure that you're in a position to get a job doing what you want, where you want, working the hours you want.

"Try to decide how long you are going to stay at home before you try to get back to work. If you have a milestone in place, you are less likely to obsess about it and have a greater chance of enjoying your time with the kids."

Stay-at-home mum of two

Make the effort to stay in touch with your previous boss. This doesn't need to be a weekly event. (In fact, they would probably find it a bit odd if you were keeping in contact every week!) An email, phone call or coffee every six months or so will help make sure they don't forget who you are. It will also allow you to keep up-to-date on what is happening in the organisation so you can spot any opportunities that come along when the time is right.

Even if your ex-boss moves to a different organisation, it's worth keeping in contact, because you never know when you may need their help in the future. And if you have a contact in a new organisation as well as your previous company, you have doubled your chances of getting noticed and hired.

During the time you're at home with your children, the industry you worked in will undoubtedly change. There is plenty that you can do to keep yourself up to date on industry developments; you can read articles and journals online, the latest books, or keep up with news by reading your industry magazine. This needn't take up a huge amount of your time; you just need to keep abreast of what is happening in your industry from time to time.

If you belong to a professional institution, it might be worth investigating maintaining your membership. Some professional institutions even offer a career break membership allowing you to stay a member for a reduced fee, to make it more affordable to keep up.

If there is another industry that you would like to break into, now is the time to start doing your research. Look out for the key trends and big issues in the area you want to move into and make sure you're aware of the changes it will face over the next few years. Think about how you could apply your skills and experience to make a contribution in your new direction.

A blank sheet of paper

If you know that going back to your previous job or profession is unrealistic for you, why not enjoy the fact that you can start again with a blank sheet of paper? You can use the time at home when you have very young children to focus on what the future might hold for you. You are in a very fortunate and unique position because you can redefine your career and use the time out to prepare yourself for a change. Here are some questions you might like to consider:

- How many hours do I want to work each week?

- How much do I need to earn to make returning to work worthwhile?

- What kind of childcare support am I likely to have in place when I return to work?

- Are there any geographical restrictions to where I can work? (For example, if you intend to work school hours, will you be able to get to school to do drop-offs and pick-ups?)

- What kind of work would I enjoy doing?

- Do I want to work for someone else or for myself?

- Could I consider retraining or doing additional qualifications so I can change careers?

- What companies do I know of that could offer the type of job and the hours I want?

- How can I start to investigate what opportunities are available?

Keep a lookout for anyone who could be useful in your quest for a job so you have some contacts when the time comes to return to work. You never know when you will come across somebody who can help you with your future job search so stay alert to possibilities. Perhaps one of your new mum friends works for an organisation in your area that offers the type of job that would interest you.

New skills

Many women decide that they don't want to return to their previous profession, industry or role. This is either because they want a change anyway or because they don't think combining their old job with a family is suitable.

While it can be challenging to fit everything in, this period at home is an ideal time to retrain or pick up new skills that will help with your job search or career change. Look at what weekend classes or evening classes are available in your local college. If there isn't anything, you could look into online/distance learning courses. These are useful because they allow you to fit your studies around your childcare and family responsibilities.

If you don't attend courses and update your skills, then the rest of your time at home is dead time, right? *Wrong!* You are still developing skills that are relevant to the workplace while caring for your children – many of which you probably aren't even aware of. When I asked the ladies who contributed to this book about what new skills they had picked up during their time at home, 99% of them said they hadn't picked up new skills, but they had drawn on the skills from their former life.

I disagree. As a stay-at-home mum, there are lots of opportunities to pick up new skills and develop your existing ones. Here is a selection for you to consider.

Time management and prioritisation

- As a mum, you often have to balance the needs of all the people in your household as well as making sure you meet some non-negotiable deadlines (e.g. feeding times and nursery pick-ups).

- You have developed efficient routines and are able to prioritise tasks (e.g. getting your older child to nursery while managing the needs of a new baby and running a house while looking after an elderly relative).

- Multitasking is now second nature and you're not quite sure what you did with all your time when you only had one task to perform at once!

Coaching and listening

- You spend your day teaching your small child about the ways of the world, encouraging them to behave responsibly and helping them navigate tricky situations and learn from them.

- You listen to other mum friends when they are in distress and help them find a way through or a solution to the situation they are facing.

Creativity

- You keep small children entertained on rainy days and may have even invented a game or two to help them pass the time.

- You have made costumes for school plays, designed posters, run a stall at the school fete or come up with ideas for fundraising.

Communication and influencing

- You've built up a new social circle and had difficult

conversations with school or nursery teachers when you felt your child was unhappy or not being dealt with appropriately.

- You've joined committees and voiced your point of view in groups.

- You've put forward ideas for fundraising or encouraged the local mums at the community centre to get together for a Christmas lunch.

Project planning

- You've organised birthday parties (found venues, organised entertainers, sent out invitations, kept track of who was attending, prepared food, prizes, party bags, managed the event on the day and roped in a team of volunteers to help make it all run smoothly).

- You've organised fundraising events for your local playgroup.

Financial management

- Having cut your income substantially and increased your outgoings, you carefully manage your household budget.

- You've managed substantial household projects, getting quotes, choosing suppliers and managing the project to make sure it stays within budget.

Crisis management

- You carry out risk assessments on an almost-constant basis, working out what situations are and are not safe for your children.

- You constantly take responsibility for the health and well-being of those around you and deal with a sick or injured child who may or may not be your own.

So as you can see, your time at home is not 'wasted'. However, you do need to think carefully about how you communicate the skills you have developed to prospective employers, if that's the route you choose to take later down the line.

CHAPTER TEN

Start Your Own Business

*"The glass ceiling that once limited a woman's
career path has paved a new road towards
business ownership, where women can utilize
their sharp business acumen while building
strong family ties."*

Erica Nicole, who left Corporate America to start YFS
Magazine

In the six years since I left the corporate world, I have seen
a shift towards more flexible working for parents. There is
a genuine desire in many organisations (both large
corporates and small businesses) to create options that
allow mothers and fathers to work the hours that are
appropriate for their family. There is still a long way to go,
however, before all employers find a way to allow parents
to make a meaningful contribution in the workplace and
still accommodate a 9am-3pm school day and 12 weeks of
school holidays a year. As a result, a lot of mums decide
that a return to paid employment just isn't compatible

with the type of family life that they want – even when their children are older.

Working for yourself

As an alternative to going back into the workplace, more and more women are now considering self-employment as a means of earning an income. In the UK, the number of self-employed women is rising rapidly: in fact, women are opting for self-employment nearly three times faster than men. There are now more than 1.2 million self-employed women working either full- or part-time. According to the Office for National Statistics, the number of female entrepreneurs increased by 9.6% between 2012 and 2014 compared to a rise of just 3.3% for men.

The increase in the number of women running a business around their family was reflected in Oxford English Dictionary's decision to enter the term 'mumpreneur' into the dictionary a couple of years ago. A mumpreneur is defined as *'a woman who combines running a business enterprise with looking after her children'*. According to Mumpreneur UK, an estimated 300,000 female entrepreneurs are mumpreneurs, collectively contributing £7.4bn to the economy each year.

However, 'mumpreneur' is a Marmite term and people either love or hate it. Some people say that mumpreneur is derogatory because you would never find a male business owner calling themselves a 'dadpreneur'. Others proudly use the term to describe the way they juggle their family and business life.

Mumpreneurs have made a decision to put their family at the heart of all that they do. They are a distinct group of businesswomen who face a unique set of challenges. They can only hold events at times that do not clash with the school run. They can only attend networking groups that either allow them to take children along or are late enough in the evening that they can get there when they are child-free. They have very limited time to build their business and need to be exceptionally focused to get results.

> *"I am so pleased with my decision to stay at home but I couldn't do it for the long term, I need to have something else in my life whether that is volunteering or earning money. I have realised that I do need 'me'-time where I can use my skills, but I've also proved that I am a good mum and having the balance between the two is exactly what I need."*
>
> Tricia, stay-at-home mum of two

In my case, I knew from the minute I found out I was pregnant that a return to my previous job would not be compatible with the type of family life that my husband and I wanted to create. As a result, I have spent the past six years since leaving the corporate world working on a variety of projects, blogging, building websites, mastering social media and building my network. This means I have gained the skills and contacts I need to grow my business and make the level of income that I want, so I don't need to return to the corporate world when Boy Wonder starts school.

If you decide to stay at home with the kids, but still want to earn an income, running your own business is certainly an option. Before you plunge in head first, though, there are a few things to consider. First, you need to be sure that being a business owner is the right setting for you. And if it is, you need to make sure that you set up the right kind of business that works for the way you run your family life.

Are you cut out to be a business owner?

Running a business is not for everyone. It takes hard work, dedication and a huge dollop of self-discipline. The entrepreneurial lifestyle provides the ultimate in freedom. You can set your own direction, decide the hours that you want to work, and the clients you want to bring in. You have nobody to answer to and are the master of your own destiny. Sounds wonderful, doesn't it?

On the flip side, you have nobody to answer to. So whether you get the work done or not, nobody will question you. You can get back from the school run, feel tired, and hop back into bed for a snooze. But if you keep that up every day, you'll never put the effort and energy required into pushing your business forward and making it the successful and profitable enterprise of your dreams.

Do you have the strategic planning ability and vision to

define the path for your business? Do you have the creativity to identify ways to market your product and build your business? Do you have the discipline to keep working on your business when you are tired and life is difficult? You need to be completely honest with yourself.

Is being the master of your own destiny all it's cracked up to be anyway? There will be no steady salary that will magically appear in your bank account every month. You're responsible for going out there and generating every penny of your income. There will be no company car, no staff discount, no pension scheme, no long service awards. It's just *you*.

If the thought of it all being down to you enthuses and motivates you, then setting up your own business is probably the right choice. But if you don't think you're cut out to be a business owner, don't force it. Running your own business is not for everyone. Just because it seems like a good way to combine a career with your family does not necessarily mean that it is the right option for you.

What kind of business is right for you?

There are two key decisions that you need to make when deciding on the type of business that you want to set up:

1. How much money do you need/want to earn from your business?

2. How much time do you want/are you able to spend developing and running your business?

Money

If you have a set amount of revenue that you **must** generate on a monthly basis, this will influence how quickly you need to get your business up and running and also the type of business that you set up. If you need to generate a return quickly, you are more likely to be successful if you draw on your existing skillset and network of contacts, and perhaps work on a freelance basis for a previous employer.

If you have more flexibility on how quickly you need to generate an income, you have more options on the type of business you can create. Your business will not be profitable overnight. You may need to make a significant upfront investment to get your enterprise off the ground. Understanding the capital required and the income projections will be key to understanding whether a business opportunity is right for you.

Time

How much time are you planning to devote to your business? Will you work around the children or will you use childcare to free up longer chunks of time that you can dedicate to working on your business?

I have spoken to many mums who are building a business and feel guilty about using childcare. After all, the whole point of not returning to work was to be there for the children. Personally, I think you need to be pragmatic. You will probably need less childcare than if you returned to your old job. You are more likely to be working closer to your childcare provider and, therefore, can be more flexible. Ultimately, you're working towards a more flexible future for your family so there is absolutely nothing to feel guilty about.

You should be realistic about the amount of income you can generate in the time that you have available though. If you're aiming to earn £50k in your first year of business and you only have nap times and evenings to do the work, you could well find this a real stretch.

Perhaps you envisage the amount of time that you are able to devote to your business steadily increasing as your children get older. In which case, you can also plan for your revenue to increase in line with the amount of time that you have available to devote to your business.

Types of self-employment to consider

There are various models of self-employment and different types of business that you can set up.

Work for your previous employer

Your ability to work flexibly for your previous employer will very much depend on your skillset and the type of work that you used to do. You may find opportunities arise that allow you to work from home either on an ad-hoc project basis or longer term. In collaboration with your employer, clearly identify the scope of the work, how often (if at all) you would be expected to go into the office and the extent to which you can be flexible with the hours you work.

Freelancing

If you're keen to continue to use your existing skills in the profession you trained for, you may find freelance work a valid option. Being freelance means you can undertake the work you are skilled in doing on a contract basis and for specific periods of time. This allows you to make a cash injection into the family budget without the long-term commitment of being employed.

Franchise

Buying a franchise is worth considering if you want to run a business but don't have a specific business idea or you prefer the security that an established concept brings. Instead of setting up a business from scratch, you use a proven business idea, usually trading under the brand name of the business that is offering the franchise to you. You have help and support from the franchise provider.

There are usually significant start-up costs involved with buying a franchise; however, this is balanced with the fact that successful franchises have a much lower failure rate than completely new businesses.

Turn your hobby into a business

If you have a particular hobby that you enjoy, it's worth

thinking about whether there is any potential to make some cash there. Perhaps you make jewellery or candles? Maybe you're an expert baker and could sell birthday cakes and cupcakes in your local area? While you won't likely get rich quick running any of these kinds of businesses, they'll certainly help you contribute to the family finances.

You could also consider sharing your expertise (say, in cookery, car maintenance, knitting, sewing... the opportunities are endless!) Why not run short courses, either for individuals or small groups? You could even offer gift certificates or sell associated products to course attendees.

Set up a service

Perhaps it appeals to you to use your existing skillset to set up a service-based business. For example:

- The market for virtual assistants (VAs) has exploded in recent years. Small businesses and solo entrepreneurs need admin support, but don't want the fixed cost of employing people permanently. Virtual assistants sell their services on a contract basis and provide the admin support that these businesses need, often remotely, working from their own home.

- You could become an eBay agent and sell items on behalf of other people. Not everyone has the time or patience to sell their goods on eBay. For many people, it can be too complicated and overwhelming. You could list items for other people and take a percentage of the sale or charge a flat fee to list on their behalf.

- Kids' parties are big business these days and many parents are too busy to spend the time planning their child's party in detail. Consider offering a full service of planning, catering and entertainment.

Try to think of services that suit your interests, skillset and schedule. If your children are very young, focus on what you can do during nap times. If you have children at preschool and nursery, think about what you can you fit in around drop-offs and pick-ups.

Sell a product

You could set up a business selling a particular product or range, either online or from a physical location.

Perhaps you have come across a product while on holiday that you think would do well in your own country. This is exactly how MicroScooters were introduced to the UK. A mum spotted them while on holiday in Switzerland and then almost by accident became the sole UK distributer of the scooters. Introducing a product to a new market requires rigorous market research and the ability to make an upfront financial investment, but it can be a great way to have a tried-and-trusted product to sell.

You can also develop your own product range by buying goods from wholesalers and selling on to your own customers. Websites such as Alibaba.com also allow you to deal with wholesalers direct, on a global basis, and you can even commission your own products to be prototyped and produced.

If you decide to sell a product, you will need to think carefully about the upfront investment required and how you will store and distribute your product.

Multi-level marketing

You'll probably have come across companies such as Forever Living, Utility Warehouse, and Stella & Dot. These are all opportunities that allow you to work for yourself on a flexible basis, but with the benefit of being part of a much bigger company.

Some of the income claims made by these companies should come with a health warning, in my view! I often see Facebook posts suggesting that you can work part-time around your family and earn £2,000 a month or more. For some people who are very established and have grown large teams themselves, that may well be the case; however, I suspect income levels for your average seller are much lower.

That said, I do think these types of companies offer a great opportunity for mums who want to work for themselves to generate an income without having to start from scratch or take on the costs of setting up their own business.

Coming up with your business idea

If you think you'd like to work for yourself, keep note of all of your ideas, no matter how trivial or silly they may seem at the time. If you happen upon an idea that you are particularly enthusiastic about, then use some of your spare time to research it. Even if you can't get started on your business immediately, you can still lay the foundations and do a lot of the planning in the meantime.

When coming up with your business idea, it has to be something that you truly believe in and most importantly are passionate about. Your passion is going to be the key to your business success. If you're not passionate about the product or service that you offer, you won't be able to generate enthusiasm among your potential customers, nor will you be able to keep yourself motivated to put in the huge amount of work required to make your business a success.

Be realistic

If you do decide to build a business around your family, be realistic about what you can get done in the time you have available. Setting up your own business around your family has never been more achievable than it is now. We are lucky to live in an age of massive technological advancement, with the internet and smartphones allowing us to be truly connected to the world at all times.

Do not underestimate the amount of work that will be

involved in starting your own business or the long-term commitment that is needed to succeed. It could take several years for your business to become profitable. You need to bear in mind that you'll have limited time to invest in the business, if you're building it around your family, which means it might take even longer for your business to generate a consistent income.

This may seem quite a depressing prospect, but I'll just reiterate that you can do a lot of the groundwork while your children are young, leaving you in a great position to build a thriving, profitable entity when they head off to school. This will offer you the flexibility of running your own business and being around for your children at the same time.

If you need to generate an income faster, it's well worth considering becoming a freelancer or opting for a ready-made business with a multi-level marketing company where a lot of the groundwork has been done for you.

"The presence of a regular pay cheque has been missed greatly. I remember shredding old pay slips when I was on bed rest with my second child and thinking how wonderful it was to have a regular amount deposited into my bank account every 30 days!"

Nicola, mum of two and My Secret Kitchen Team Leader

Building a successful and profitable business around your family can be the ultimate way to combine income generation and family time simultaneously. Lots of mums are working exceptionally hard, but also reaping the rewards of building a business around their family. And you can too.

CHAPTER ELEVEN

And This Too Shall Pass...

"Being a martyr is highly overrated."

Patricia Briggs

When we look for advice on how to appear more confident and successful, very often we're told to 'fake it till we make it'. We need to think about what we want to achieve, act 'as if' we are already successful in that area and very soon we will no longer be 'faking it'. That state will be real and we will have 'made it'.

I don't believe that you can fake it till you make it when you stay home with the kids, though; the situation either works for you or it doesn't.

*"You need to do what is right for **your** family but you also need to be a bit selfish and think about yourself when making your decision. If you're happy and fulfilled then your family will be too. Your children are not going to need you 24/7 for long, so*

Some people will feel inspired, privileged and (dare I say it?) 'blessed' to be at home with their children. Others will feel suffocated, hemmed-in and irritated on a daily basis. And that's okay – after all, we're all different. Just because you made a decision to be at home at one point doesn't mean that you need to stick with it if it doesn't work for you. It's alright to say, "I tried it but it really wasn't for me."

Despite what others say, taking time out of from work does not make you unemployable. If your time at home is not working out as you planned, there are alternatives. You can simply find childcare and go back to work. No decision is ever set in stone.

Please, please don't be a martyr and think, "My children need me; I could never leave them". More than anything else, children need a happy home. That could mean a mum who's around to look after them all day every day, or it could mean a mum who goes out to work and comes back a happier and more fulfilled person.

Don't try to fake it. Otherwise, everybody loses. You miss out on having a career that fulfils you and your kids miss out on having a mum who is genuinely happy.

Identify what fulfils you

There are lots of different types of stay-at-home mums. There's the mum who wants to be around while her children are young and then return to her career when her children are old enough to go to school. There is the enterprising mum who wants to set up her own business around her family. There is the mum who wants to devote herself to her family full time and not return to paid employment at all.

Fulfilment means different things to different people. Identify what you need to be fulfilled and don't feel pressured to conform to a model that doesn't work for you.

And this too shall pass

Quite early on in my parenthood journey, I adopted a mantra that many experienced mothers told me: '…and this too shall pass'.

When you're trying to comfort a colicky baby who will *not stop crying* no matter what you do, just hold them close and silently recite to yourself '…and this too shall pass'.

When you have a little person waking you for the fifth time in one night, screaming in agony with a molar cutting through, you will comfort them the best you can, try to forget how painfully sleep-deprived you are and silently recite to yourself '…and this too shall pass'.

When you have a toddler screaming on the supermarket floor and you can feel the disapproving stares of other shoppers, you will deal with the situation as best you can and silently recite to yourself '…and this too shall pass'.

When a pre-schooler comes out of nursery sobbing because she wasn't picked to be the special helper today and nothing you do will console her, you will distract her with her favourite book and silently recite to yourself '…and this too shall pass'.

And lovely lady, it will indeed pass.

When you have a child, it feels as if somebody is slowing down the days but fast-forwarding the years. On the one hand, you can't remember life before your little ones came along. But on the other, every stage they go through seems to pass in the blink of an eye. So, yes, when those challenging moments arise, you can rest assured that '…this too shall pass'. But, sadly, so too will all of the incredible moments:

- Like when your baby seeks you out in a crowded

room and gives you the biggest, beamiest glowing smile when your eyes meet.

- Like when your toddler comforts an upset friend and offers them her toy in the hope that it makes her feel better.

- Like when you attend your first nativity play and you nervously wait for your donkey to take the stage, and hope beyond hope that he manages to hold it together and doesn't get scared or burst into tears.

- Like when your school-age child bounds out of school and throws her arms around you shouting "Mummy!" and you know that, without a doubt, no matter how much fun she has had with her friends, this is absolutely the best part of her day.

All of these moments will pass. The clock is ticking. You can't press rewind and live through them again. You've got to grab them while you can because you won't have a second chance to live these moments.

In 2012, when the Olympics came to London, I was at home caring for a three-year-old and a six-month-old. I knew a couple of people who had worked on the campaign to bring the Olympics to London and throughout the Games I had an uneasy feeling. People I'd worked with, who once upon a time were my peers in Corporateland, had put their heart and soul into making these Games happen.

Hundreds upon hundreds of amazing athletes had

dedicated years of their life to prepare for a life-changing event. The country was swept up in a haze of Olympic glory and I felt that I was missing out. So many people were 'out there' doing great work and making a difference. What was I doing?

I was changing nappies and cooking meals that were rejected on a daily basis. I was walking on eggshells trying not to upset a stroppy toddler and my life was dictated by the mood and demands of two small people who had me pretty much at their beck and call. What was I doing with my life? What was my contribution?

At the closing ceremony, Lord Sebastian Coe told the world:

> *"On the first day of these Games, I said we were determined to do it right. I said that these Games would see the best of us. On this last day, I can conclude with these words: when our time came, Britain, we did it right. Thank you!"*

And at that moment, it all slotted into place for me.

When Super Girl was born, I promised her that I would 'do it right'. That I would be there to look after her, protect her from the world and help her to be anything she wanted to be and do anything she wanted to do.

When my time came to be a mum, I believe that (at least to date) I 'did it right'. I did not do what is right for you or your sister or your friend or your colleague. I did what was right for me and my family.

I can't guarantee that my children have always seen the best of me. I've got a quick temper and patience is not my strong point. But they have always known that they are loved, protected and safe. And one thing is for certain. With every day that passes, our little people are getting bigger and bigger. They're going to become increasingly independent and build a life of their own. There is going to come a time when mum is not the first person they call for when they are hurt, when mum is not the person they want to share their day with and when they don't sneak into bed for an early morning cuddle.

Staying home with the kids can be hard, especially when you had a 'life' before they came along. The day-to-day care of your children is relentless and monotonous. And while it might not feel like it sometimes (or even a lot of the time!) I genuinely believe that for my family I am 'doing it right'.

If you're trying to decide whether staying home with the kids is right for you and your family, by all means weigh up the pros and cons, but before you make that final decision, listen to that little voice in your head. What is it telling you to do? Listen to it, because it's usually right.

Decided to stay at home with your kids? Then I salute you, lovely lady. You are not alone. There are lots of us out here doing the best we can for our family. Lots. As a result, we are experiencing extraordinary moments every day in very ordinary circumstances.

It's hard work, but if we do it right, when our children are older and we're looking back on our life, we'll have no regrets. At least when it comes to how we looked after our little people. And that is something pretty special.

Nicola Semple, is a mum of two who passionately wants women to feel empowered and able to create the family life that works for them.

BC (Before Children), she was a management consultant working with large corporate and private sector clients. Now she uses her business skills to help mums build a successful and profitable business from home.

Nicola is a displaced Glaswegian, living in Surrey, England. (You can take the girl out of Glasgow, but you'll never take Glasgow out of the girl.) She lives with her Surinamese Dutch husband and two little people. When not on the school run or spending endless hours in swing parks and soft play, she can be found working one-to-one mentoring clients and running online training programmes to help mums find focus, skills and direction to rock their business their way.

Nicola has been featured in *The Green Parent*, *The Guardian*, *The Business Mums Journal* and was the winner of Work For Mums Marvellous Mumpreneur Award in 2013.

Want to find out more about Nicola? Head to http://nicolasemple.com

Or connect with her:

By email: nicola@nicolasemple.com

On Facebook: NicolaSemplePage

On Twitter: @nsemple

Printed in Great Britain
by Amazon